W9-CYY-239

DATE DUE

WITHDRAWN

THE LUNTS
by George Freedley

THE LUNTS

by

GEORGE FREEDLEY

*An illustrated study of their work, with a
list of their appearances on stage and screen*

THE MACMILLAN COMPANY
NEW YORK
1958

122278

This book is affectionately and apprecia-
tively dedicated to the glamorous and
delightful subjects of this little biography,
Lynn Fontanne and Alfred Lunt

Theatre World Monographs
GENERAL EDITOR : FRANCES STEPHENS
CONSULTANT AND PICTURE EDITORS:
RAYMOND MANDER AND JOE MITCHENSON

Printed in Great Britain
by CHARLES BIRCHALL AND SONS, LTD., LIVERPOOL AND LONDON

CONTENTS

ACKNOWLEDGMENTS

The Author wishes to thank William Heinemann Ltd. and Doubleday and Co. for permission to quote the lines from Noël Coward's *Present Indicative*. He also wishes to thank Theresa Helburn and Lawrence Langner of the Theatre Guild, George Greenberg, Bob Downing, Donald Buka and others who have worked with the Lunts, for their stories. For script assistance thanks are due to Ed Burke and Gordon Ericksen. For pictures and research he wishes to thank Florence Vandamm, Raymond Mander, Joe Mitchenson, Ed Burke, Gordon Ericksen, the late Francis Brugiere, the White Studios, and particularly his wonderful staff at the Theatre Collection of the New York Public Library.

The Editors wish to thank *Picture Show* Library for the loan of film stills and *Theatre World* for the use of their files.

ILLUSTRATIONS

7

THE LUNTS

I

S L I M , willowy Lynn was born in England at Woodford in the lovely county of Essex, the daughter of Jules Pierre Antoine Fontanne and his wife, Frances Ellen Thornley, in the days of a prosperous England with doughty Victoria safe on her imperial throne in the sun which never set on her domain. In those days there were small, limited wars which mostly concerned military families and their men. In thriving London the West End playhouses were crowded with comedies which with almost no exceptions have disappeared from the boards, and problem plays *à la* Pinero which spread from London to New York, but today mean nothing. It was, however, a period of fine, even great, acting and Lynn was fortunate to be able to see and later, as she grew up, to study with one of the truly great ones.

But that was not yet. Life in the country was pleasant; travel abroad was easy with few passport difficulties. Countries wanted to be visited and made life as comfortable as possible for travellers—even the Customs, except the United States, of course, but Lynn hadn't travelled there yet.

Her father was born in England of French parentage from a family which originated near Lyons. Mr. Fontanne was a printer and inventor in which profession he prospered. He met and married Frances Thornley, the lovely daughter of a nice upper-middle-class family, and she bore him four daughters. Only one was to come to great fame but all of them were beautiful.

During her early schooling in Essex she became imbued with the idea of becoming an actress. Her ideal was Ellen Terry who had been sublime in comedy and tragedy alike and who had for thirty years partnered and co-starred with Sir Henry Irving. Miss Terry had left Irving and played with her own company in London and New York, but she had begun to accept a few talented pupils. Lynn was sponsored by Miss Ada Heatherbigg, a friend of Lynn's mother. Miss Terry thought that the child had unusual talent and kept her as a pupil for many months. She sometimes had Lynn to stay with her at her cottage at Smallhythe in Kent.

Ellen Terry had extraordinary charm, sweetness, kindness, natural gaiety and a great gift with children. She taught Lynn to walk with a sheet pinned to her front and another to her back trailing twelve inches along the floor. She taught her to walk with these encumbrances forwards and backwards and to the sides. She taught Lynn the interpretation of King Lear's Cordelia which she herself had played with Sir Henry Irving. She said to her, "*Think* of the *meaning* of what you are saying and let the words pour out of your mouth." Miss Terry was a realistic actress, absolutely truthful.

Dame Ellen, as she later became, quite wisely decided that the best thing in the world for Lynn was to be thrust into a big musical pantomime production where she would become accustomed to the hurly-burly back stage at the Theatre Royal, Drury Lane. No provincial or suburban pantomimes for her pupil, opined Miss Terry. Let her start at the top as well as at the bottom. There she would learn of the world of stage hands and stars, the famous interpreters of Christmas pantomimes. She would learn how to get along with other girls back stage who were just as ambitious as she was. Armed with Ellen Terry's precious letter to Arthur Collins, the manager of the famous Theatre Royal, Drury Lane, Lynn paid her first call on a manager. The note testified to her acting ability, and her brunette hair and cameo-like face showed her beauty to those who cared to look. Mr. Collins looked —and engaged her to be one of his young ladies in his forthcoming Christmas pantomime.

Lynn was naturally bewildered at first, but soon got on to the routine. It was exciting and thrilling even to be just one of the girls in a big pantomime. She was on stage and back stage in the venerable playhouse which had behind it over 200 years of history. When Lynn was asked her impressions of that first appearance in pantomime, her first and last as it turned out to be, she said, "Why, I was on stage—any stage-struck child knows what that means." She remembers on opening night, while marching around in a queue of little pages, saying to herself in time to the music, "I'm on the stage. I'm on the stage."

The time came, however, for the pantomime season to end, so Lynn began the rounds of managers' offices and soon achieved walk-ons in support of such stars as Lewis Waller, Lena Ashwell and the distinguished actor-producer, Herbert Beerbohm Tree, half-brother of the great caricaturist and writer, Max Beerbohm. When she wasn't rehearsing or performing, she haunted managers' offices and was finally rewarded with the part of Rose in the touring company of Somerset Maugham's delightful *Lady*

Frederick. A year later she achieved her first West End speaking part as Lady Mulberry in *Billy's Bargain,* with Weedon Grossmith, "not much of a part in not much of a play" she recalls.

However, attaining the tiny part gave her confidence. It was a great advance over pantomime and all those walk-ons and also it was in London in 1910, a very good time to be alive there and acting, no matter how indifferent the role. Next she was offered a chance by Grossmith to join the company going to America of a routine comedy, *Mr. Preedy and the Countess,* in which she had toured earlier in the year, and accepted it at once. She would see America, which might prove rewarding. It did, but much later, for her first play lingered on Broadway a paltry three weeks and soon she was back in London looking for a part in a play. She remained with Weedon Grossmith and his company in London and on tour until she had her first real chance as Gertrude Rhead, a spinster role with great possibilities, in a touring company of *Milestones,* the big success by Edward Knoblock and Arnold Bennett which was then running at the Royalty Theatre. With this company she spent the whole of the spring and autumn of 1913. For the first time she had a leading role and was rewarded by glowing notices up and down the country.

Ellen Terry, who had taught her and given her that precious letter of introduction which had unlocked the stage door for her, remained her dear friend. Another great friend of this period was young Edith Evans, now a Dame and reigning queen of the London stage. Another friend was Harcourt Williams, actor and director, long a Bensonian, as members of Sir F. R. Benson's Shakespearean company were affectionately known. Williams had once toured with Ellen Terry which made him even more the friend. Later on he became a bulwark of the Old Vic Company. Edmund Goulding, the playwright and later a Hollywood mogul, was another friend of that period. Her more intimate friends were Wilfred de Glehns for whom she posed many times (incidentally his wife was Robert E. Sherwood's aunt), and Roger Quilter, the composer. All of these were friends of John Singer Sargeant, the great American portrait painter.

After the long tour of *Milestones* the same management brought her to London where she appeared in two parts, Mrs. Collison and Liza in Edward Knoblock's *My Lady's Dress* at the Royalty in 1914. One notice read: "Miss [Gladys] Cooper gives a pathetic study of a hump-backed girl with a selfish sister whom Miss Lynn Fontanne enacts to the life." Dennis Eadie, Edith Evans, Beryl Mercer and Edmund Goulding were also in the cast.

In fairness to Lynn's development into a great actress, it must be recorded that she was chastised as well as praised in the early days.

She had been so effective in *My Lady's Dress* that when it was decided to revive *Milestones* later in the year she was given the opportunity of again playing Gertrude Rhead. Her notices were disappointing in London, although it was evident that she was rising in the theatre.

That great American actress, Laurette Taylor, comedy queen and later creator of dramatic roles, was in London at the time and saw her in both Knoblock plays. They actually met at a party given for charity. In 1916 Laurette sent for her to come to America to act in a series of plays she planned to do.

She joined Laurette's company in Rochester, New York, in the tryout of J. Hartley Manners' *The Harp of Life* in March 1916, which Manners had created especially for his wife, Miss Taylor. In November the show opened on Broadway and Lynn's second appearance in New York City was well received. "But next to Miss Taylor's the outstanding performance of the evening is given by Miss Lynn Fontanne, who played a bit in *My Lady's Dress* in London, caught Miss Taylor's eye and was brought here by her. She plays the girl Sylvia had picked for her boy, and it is a notably direct, eloquent, and moving performance. You will enjoy it among other things—many other things—in *The Harp of Life*."[1] ". . . and in Lynn Fontanne, an appallingly gowned young woman who wore plum colored shoes during all the evening, the audience found a character to regard with the warmest applause. In all that she said and did she was one of the few recognizable humans on the stage." [2]

"One of the delights of the performance is the exquisite acting of a newcomer, Lynn Fontanne, who established a reputation for uncommon ability overnight. Miss Fontanne comes from England, and it is earnestly hoped that she never returns."[3]

In the spring of 1917 she appeared as "Princess" Lizzie in *Out There*, by Manners again. Her reception is herein recorded: "The acting is of a high order throughout, with Lynn Fontanne again illustrating her remarkable aptitude for characterization in the role of the unpleasant sister. . ."[4]

[1] *New York Times*, 28 November 1916.
[2] The *Sun*, 28 November 1916.
[3] Rennold Wolf, *Morning Telegraph*, 28 November 1916.
[4] *New York Dramatic Mirror*, 7 April 1917.

The next offering of the Laurette Taylor company saw her as Winifred in Manners' *The Wooing of Eve* the next season at the Criterion. Then came the same author's *Happiness* with Lynn again getting good notices and indicating progress. ". . . and Lynn Fontanne, a capital actress gifted with genuine versatility, played the lachrymose cousin with exceedingly good humorous effect."[1]

"As the weeping and willowy bride, Lynne Fontaine [sic] also decked herself in laurels, though no orange blossoms were hers. The comedy of tears is pushed to the verge of farce, but Miss Fontaine's instinct is so true and her methods so sure that she is endlessly delightful—really an extraordinary performance."[2]

About her performance in *Happiness* they wrote: "Lynn Fontaine [sic] shows a marvellous [sic] sense of caricature in the part of an irresponsible chattering spinster,"[3] and "Lynn Fontanne does a capital bit of work as a hair-brained social waster."[4]

Early in April 1918, during World War I, she appeared as Bianca to Laurette's Katherine in *The Taming of the Shrew* in *Scenes from Shakespeare* and as Nerissa to her Portia. Her fresh English beauty and superior diction were much admired. This was her first "go" at the Bard, but these first appearances were in the back of her mind when she essayed Beatrice later in the never-to-open *Much Ado About Nothing* and made her real triumph as Katherine in *The Shrew* seventeen years later. *Much Ado* was abandoned in rehearsal because the Theatre Guild officers felt that Robert Edmond Jones' scheme of

[1] *New York World*, 10 November 1917.
[2] *New York Times*, 10 November 1917.
[3] Louis Sherwin, *Globe*, New York, 4 January 1918.
[4] Charles Darnton, *New York Evening World*, 2 January 1918.

direction was ineffective. The acting was approved, but the production was called off.

Miss Fontanne's first role in an Eugene O'Neill play was in March, 1920, in Philadelphia in *Chris*. The play was not ready for Broadway and it was withdrawn for script revisions. However, the press in Philadelphia did well by our star. "Lynn Fontanne, charming in her young womanhood and in complete sympathy with the role of the daughter, won deserved admiration."[1] "Lynn Fontanne as the daughter, 'Anna Christophersen', was again seen in an ingenue role, which she played charmingly— a young girl with some decision of character and the attractiveness of serious girlhood."[2]

Re-written, this play became *Anna Christie* which in 1921 made Pauline Lord a star, but Lynn was already winning Chicago hearts as Dulcinea in *Dulcy* in its pre-Broadway tour. After the closing of *Chris,* she had rejoined Laurette's company and travelled with them to London to appear in Manners' *One Night in Rome* at the Garrick in May, 1920. Heckling and a riot broke out in the gallery. Laurette fled from the stage sobbing hysterically. The story has been told often by Laurette, by C. B. Cochran, the manager, and others. Lynn says: "I'm afraid we got the worst of it, Greta Kemble-Cooper and Barry Baxter and I, because we came on after an interesting scene which had had the audience's attention, but ours was rather dull. Then the spectators remembered that they were annoyed with Laurette, with Cochran, and Hartley's play. So they vented their irritation by hurling stink bombs. We stood it as long as we could. Finally

[1] *Philadelphia Record,* 16 March 1920.
[2] *Philadelphia Press,* 16 March 1920

Cochran walked on, after we had retired with streaming eyes, and led on Laurette. She sobbed slightly and effectively, and said, 'This is not awfully like England', and Cockie led her off."

Lynn also remembered that she recovered sufficiently from the debacle to realize that the curtain rang down at 9.30 p.m. and she could go to the party which she had previously declined because she was acting. She naturally was the centre of attention. After all, she was an attractive girl with NEWS and who would resist the combination! The play, damaged by the disastrous opening, barely eked out its 104 performances, but Lynn was back in London and could see her friends again; however, she was called back to America to get her first real chance in *Dulcy*, as the young bride who tries to help out her husband and only puts her foot in her mouth. Her Dulcy-isms written by Marc Connelly and George S. Kaufman became as famous and as widely repeated as Mala-propisms, and since Dulcinea was much younger and prettier than Sheridan's comedienne, adoring audiences cheered her. "The first medal for shaking the shaker belongs to Lynn Fontanne. This is an exceedingly merry performance. The humor of a young woman supposed to be a deadly bore might actually become so in less skillful hands, but Miss Fontanne preserves the spirit of mockery and the authors have been wise enough to let the bromides swirl into drifts."[1]

"The debt to Lynn Fontanne is greater. As Dulcinea, she is brilliant—no less. This English player has been with us several seasons, making her first appearance in *The Harp of Life* and then, unforgettably, in *Out There*.

[1] Heywood Broun, *New York Tribune*, 15 August 1921.

THE LUNTS

Always she has played with Laurette Taylor, whom now, in a hundred tricks of gesture and tones of voice, she most uncannily resembles. It was apparent from the first that she was an actress of uncommon quality, and not even the rich role of Dulcy which offers her her first full-size opportunity, measures up to her suspected stature. She can do great things and perhaps she will."[1]

In May 1923 she played Lady Castlemaine and Laurette Taylor played Nell in a revival of Paul Kester's *Sweet Nell of Old Drury*. What is of particular interest is the fact that Alfred Lunt (through the courtesy of Distguished Films Inc.) played Charles II. It was the first time that they had played together although off-stage they were married. This revival took place at the 48th Street Theatre.

"Lynn Fontanne was the superb though flouted Lady Castlemaine—a part whole worlds removed from her delectable moron, Dulcy, yet as perfect in every accent, lineament and gesture. She had even a bit of the 'authority' which Miss Taylor sometimes lacked, carrying off the crude lines of her part with the distinction of an old master. . . . . The men did not come off so well. That admirable comedian, Alfred Lunt was well nigh submerged in the costume and in the dummy personality of this Charles Rex."

In August 1923 Lynn went into Vincent Lawrence's *In Love with Love* with Ralph Morgan, Henry Hull and Berton Churchill. "The part of Anne is more nearly 'straight' than any Miss Fontanne has attempted and gives only partial scope to her great powers of whimsical and original characterization. . . . This is a new note in

[1] Alexander Woollcott, *New York Times*, 15 August 1921.

Miss Fontanne's scale and one that is destined to delight many hearts, for the success of *In Love with Love* is never for a moment in doubt."[1]

II

A L F R E D L U N T was born in Milwaukee, Wisconsin, the son of Alfred Lunt and his wife, Harriet Washburn Briggs. He was a descendant of a New England family and there is no Scandinavian blood as rumoured, a theory given weight by his superb portrayal of a Finnish professor in *There Shall Be No Night*. Various newspaper stories have appeared which state that Alfred was born with the name "Ecklund". Someone had told him that he was so listed in the catalogue of the Theatre Collection of the New York Public Library. On 25 June 1956 he wrote me in part that he understood "that on my 'card' I am listed as Alfred Lunt (real name, Ecklund) or something like that. Not true. I was born Alfred Davis Lunt Jr. and am as Yankee as can be. My father was born in Orono, Maine in 1830 (yes 1830) and my mother was born in Hortonville, Wisconsin in 1862. My step-father was a Finnish-Swede which may account for a lot of the confusion."

Young Lunt was stage-struck at an early age as his scrapbook of clippings and pictures of performers on the Milwaukee stage testify. He saw every play his parents permitted him to attend and that his juvenile pocketbook could afford when not substantially assisted from parental sources.

[1] John Corbin, *New York Times*, 7 August 1923.

19

Alfred received his preliminary schooling in Milwaukee and later was educated at Carroll College in Waukesha, Wisconsin. He states that he "went to Boston to enter the Emerson School of Oratory (it was my dramatic teacher's school) to prepare for the theatre, but attended only one day as on the following day I passed the Castle Square Theatre, stopped in, and asked for a job and got it.

"I opened two days later as the Sheriff in James Montgomery's *The Aviator*. I stayed on for three years playing bits and small parts at five dollars a week for the first month and then twenty dollars."

John Parker's *Who's Who in the Theatre* still states that he went to Harvard, which is not correct, though had he attended, he would have had the opportunity of participating in George Pierce Baker's famous "47 Workshop". But he was certainly learning the acting profession under the astute actor-manager, E. E. Clive.

In 1913 Lunt joined the Canadian-born Margaret Anglin's company and acted with her for eighteen months in *Beverly's Balances, Green Stockings, As You Like It*, among other plays on tour. Miss Anglin was known for drama and tragedy as well as comedy, in all of which she excelled. In 1915, he appeared in her support in the celebrated open-air Greek Theatre at the University of California at Berkeley in *Iphigenia in Tauris* and *Medea*. He found himself transferred from the blue California skies to the vaudeville circuit as leading man to the declining and full-blown Lily Langtry in a playlet by Percy Fendall entitled *Ashes*. He toured with Miss Anglin again the next year. It was not until October 1917 that he made his Broadway debut as Claude Estabrook in *Romance and Arabella*. Charles Darnton in the *Evening World* mentions "Alfred Lunt, as the Greenwich Village free-lover who did capital work".

Alfred, after *Romance and Arabella*, toured in *The Country Cousin* with considerable success. His performance was witnessed and admired by Booth Tarkington who recognized a great comic talent when he saw one. Because of this, he wrote *Clarence*—which was tailored for Alfred.

In 1919, playing the title-role in *Clarence*, he made a great hit portraying the bumbling ex-soldier to the hilt to gain much critical praise. "Alfred Lunt, one of our most artistic comedians, carries off the acting honors in the role of Clarence. He is, without question, the most capable of all the players who have portrayed a Tarkington character on the stage".[1]

"Alfred Lunt gave a most amusing performance of the entomologist, making the physical manifestations of the character broadly grotesque. He seemed at times to adopt the dramatic method of the experienced Bert Williams, even in his gait and his furtive and worried look."[2]

He played Clarence for two years and then came another droll Tarkington comedy, *The Intimate Strangers* with Billie Burke. "Alfred Lunt, recently of *Clarence* and much more avoirdupoiser than he was in those days, was an admirable foil for Miss Burke. A better and more satisfactory leading man could never have been secured. I had been wondering if Mr. Lunt was too good an actor to be in demand, and it was a pleasure to meet him again. Sometimes the actors who have achieved one success vanish curiously."[3]

[1] Louis Gardy in the *New York Call*.
[2] The *Sun*, 22 September 1919.
[3] Alan Dale, *New York American*, 8 November 1921.

21

"Alfred Lunt, playing the bachelor, repeats a few of the tricks that gave an original touch to his 'Clarence' two seasons back, but seem a bit forced in the new play. Otherwise he is a mannerly and capable actor." [1]

"Alfred Lunt as the New York lawyer who took seriously his not-too-many years gave a performance of equal quality. It was a deft bit of comedy acting with its suggestion of good manners, half credulity and embarrassed mystification." [2]

After having watched each other on stage and having met at parties, Lynn and Alfred found they liked being around each other. They were both part of that great theatrical family which centered at the Algonquin Hotel, later at Sardi's and other theatrical rendezvous, many of which are gone and merely remote news to today's theatre crowd of which the Lunts are very much a part, although their public appearances are naturally spaced. They had many friends in common, including a young compatriot of Lynn's, Noël Coward, but when it came time for them to take their fateful plunge into Holy Matrimony, they consulted no one. They simply took the subway to City Hall on a Friday morning, 26 May 1922, when both were safely ensconced in hit shows. They knew they were meant for each other for ever. (They celebrated their thirty-fifth anniversary in New York while this narrative was being written.) They arrived at City Hall and found two strangers and asked them to be witnesses. They smilingly agreed. Alfred reached in his pocket to pay the fee and came up with a little change but no bills. Lynn fumbled in her pocketbook with similar embarrassing

[1] Burns Mantle, *New York Mail*, 8 November 1921.
[2] Louis V. DeFoe, *New York World*, 8 November 1921.

results. Reluctantly Alfred borrowed the necessary amount from one of the witnesses. That is how they became Mr. and Mrs. Alfred Lunt and were back at their respective theatres that evening. It was a decision that they have never regretted. It is one of the happiest private and professional marriages that the theatre has ever known. Friends come and go. Other marriages collapse, as the gossip columns relate. Scandal touches others but the Lunts remain a pair undivided.

In September 1922 his role of Count Alexandre de Lussac in *Banco,* Clare Kummer's adaptation from the French of Alfred Savoir, was somewhat sensational, that of an inveterate gambler who lost a wife because of his addiction and regained her also because of it. "Alfred Lunt begins the play with a very bad attack of mannerisms. All through the first act he is some sort of boyish Puck with knotted face and tense body. He improves steadily toward the close when he is really very good."[1]

"Alfred Lunt without the visible effort and the fiddle-dee-dee mannerisms with which he has been hobbling himself. . ."[2] "After seeing *Banco* last night I have the opinion that Mr. Lunt is pre-eminent among American players, in acting such Parisian characters as may be entitled Count Alexandre de Lussac."[3]

However, *Banco* did not keep him occupied for long, so that he was available for the before-mentioned Equity Players' revival of *Sweet Nell of Old Drury* the following spring.

After this play closed and Lynn went into *In Love with Love,* Alfred waited until October for John Drinkwater's

[1] Kenneth Macgowan, *New York Globe,* 21 September 1922.
[2] Alexander Woollcott, *New York Times,* 21 September 1922.
[3] Percy Hammond, *New York Tribune,* 21 September 1922.

Robert E. Lee, the long expected companion-piece to his *Abraham Lincoln* which had been widely acclaimed. Alfred played a young Southern soldier to the Canadian Berton Churchill as General Lee. William Harris, Jr. opened this paean to a great American and beloved Southerner in Richmond, the capital of the Confederacy, with a mixed cast of Northerners. The audience frankly couldn't understand much of the English spoken on stage, particularly the stage English of Marse Bob. The riot of protest that broke out did not occur in the Academy of Music but in the drawing-rooms and even earlier in the newspaper offices of a deeply offended Richmond. Douglas Southall Freeman, the distinguished Pulitzer Prize author of the four-volume biography of Lee, was also the editor of the *Richmond News-Leader.* He appointed himself subsidiary drama critic on that occasion. The various libraries, museums and historical societies of Virginia had been excited when they learned that the great Drinkwater was to attempt a play on General Lee. They wrote offering their resources for research, for atmosphere at least. Drinkwater replied tartly and undiplomatically that "he could create his own atmosphere". The fat was in the fire and Dr. Freeman attended the opening and listened with indignation, of course, but keeping a keen ear open for the playwright's "atmosphere". The next afternoon he detailed, more or less, 253 major errors in fact, and Richmonders were even more incensed. Alfred recalled a minor mishap of that misbegotten opening at the Academy of Music in Richmond. He is always emotionally affected when the band plays "Dixie". He always wants to cry. Harold Vermilyea, who was playing one of the four Southern lads along with

1914 Royalty Theatre, London : Liza in *My Lady's Dress*, with Beryl Mercer
(Mrs. Moss) and Gladys Cooper (Annie)

1914 Royalty Theatre, London : Mrs. Collisson in *My
Lady's Dress*, with Lyston Lyle (Sir Charles)

1916 Lyceum Theatre, Rochester, New York : Winifred in *The Wooing of Eve,* with Violet Kemble Cooper (Mrs. Rodd) and Laurette Taylor (Miss Alverstone)

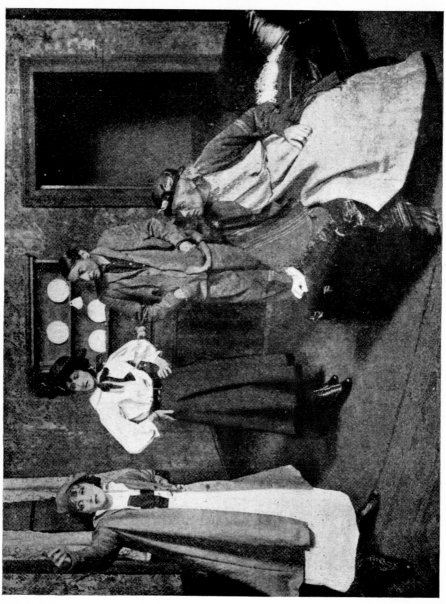

1917 Globe Theatre, New York: 'Princess' Lizzie (centre), with Laurette Taylor ('aunted Annie) (L.), Colin Campbell ('erb) and Daisy Belmore ('Old Velvet')

1921   Frazee Theatre, New York : Dulcinea in *Dulcy*

Alfred, went dry in an early scene and couldn't remember a line. He whispered to Alfred, asking for his next one. All the help he got was a low sob from the much-moved actor because "Dixie" was being played off stage, "I do-oon't kno-ow."

The poor actors had to bear the brunt of the outburst. The play moved to Broadway where it was dismissed as drama quite without regard for its historical inaccuracies. Drinkwater quite wisely kept himself at home. Richmond had quipped that undoubtedly Drinkwater would open his then projected *Stonewall Jackson* in Boston where Virginians were sure it would have more sympathetic audiences. The Lee drama closed at the Ritz Theatre after fifteen performances.

Next came Alfred's first serious success as the attractive young wastrel, Tom Prior, in Sutton Vane's imaginative play about "halfways", *Outward Bound,* in January 1924, also at the Ritz. The cast was superb and included Beryl Mercer, Dudley Digges, Margalo Gillmore, Leslie Howard, Lionel Watts, Eugene Powers, J. M. Kerrigan and Charlotte Greenville. "Mr. Lunt finds large scope for his powers as a comedian and finally does a bit of emotional acting of the very first order."[1]

"In such a play, there is need of inspired and imaginative acting and no cast of the season has been so consistently fine as that which plays *Outward Bound.* Perhaps there is reason to single out Alfred Lunt, since he has the important job of setting the mood at the very beginning."[2]

The play ran out the season, but certainly did not

[1] John Corbin, *New York Times,* 7 January 1924.
[2] Heywood Broun, *New York World,* 8 January 1924.

achieve the length of run of the 1938 revival with Laurette Taylor and Florence Reed. Broadway was not geared to the long runs of today. Now we are afflicted willy-nilly with a smash or flop policy due to the enormous production costs to get the curtain up, and to what is much more dangerous, the high operating costs of starring or even non-starring vehicles. Up until World War II it was possible to pay off the production costs in 100 performances, which was why *Variety,* the theatrical trade paper, used the term the "Century Mark" to indicate hit status. Now even if a production has run a year, but has not paid off its production costs, it is termed a flop.

III

A L F R E D   A N D   L Y N N had the excitement and satisfaction of playing together for the first time since their marriage in *Sweet Nell of Old Drury.* They were just ripe for the offer from the Theatre Guild, a producing organization which sprang from off-Broadway to the Main Stem with great success, to play the starring roles in *The Guardsman.* Both of them had had comfortable runs in separate plays, but when the opportunity came to play together and in two such spectacular parts, it was a dream come true. They knew that the Ferenc Molnar play had been produced indifferently on Broadway in 1913 in a mediocre translation and had been a failure, but with Philip Moeller as director, they felt sure enough of themselves to accept Theresa Helburn's, and the

30

Guild's invitation. (Theresa Helburn was later to become the executive director of the Theatre Guild.) They also knew that an obscure play agent had the rights to the play and was holding out for recognized Broadway stars. Lawrence Langner, another Guild director, recalls that they had to give away another section of their producers' percentage to do the play with the Lunts. "But Terry wanted them. She'd had an inspiration about them and what an inspiration it proved to be."

They also heard from Langner, who was always the expansionist at the Guild, of the plans for a permanent acting company, which was to be divided into two troupes operating in separate theatres and presenting alternating plays, which excited them. This offered them the chance to grow as actors and achieve some of the heights to which they aspired.

The Guardsman, under Moeller's suave direction which smoothed out the imperfections of the translation, opened at the Garrick Theatre *cold* as was the Guild custom with the exception of the invited Sunday night audience, as Guild openings were always on Monday nights in those days because their subscription audiences were accustomed to attending the plays on the same night of the week. Dudley Digges played the Critic, and the unforgettable and indefatigable Helen Westley was wonderfully vulgar and homely as "Mama". The run of this play almost doubled the number of performances of any play that the Lunts had appeared in separately. Was this a happy omen? They took it as such and it has never failed them. Year after year they have been asked to revive the play, even with certain revisions by Molnar to tighten rather loose situations. Knowing the slightness of the play,

31

why should they walk the tightrope again?—and they have steadfastly refused.

They did do it once again but this was for the cinema in 1931, and we are all grateful to the films that they have preserved this performance. Roland Young brought his apparently absent-minded acerbity to the Critic and was even more impassive and amusing than Digges, although both performances were excellent. Helen Westley was "naughty" in the film version as well as the stage.

Of the stage version it was said: "Alfred Lunt as the jealous actor and Lynn Fontanne as the wife who is too keen for his masquerading self are a comedy pair who need fear no compare. Their swift transition from the spats and dissension of an afternoon in their dear little home to the flirtatious byplay of the evening at the opera is wonderfully smooth and complete, and they rise most happily to the moment of confounding revelations in the third act."[1]

"Lynn Fontanne portrayed the actress often delightfully with now and again a kind of prima donna charm and no little technical fluency; she could heighten to advantage her whole performance and give it more brilliance and point. Alfred Lunt's acting was less convincing. His natural turn for cues and transitions often helped him out, but he fell a long way short of both Lynn Fontanne and Dudley Digges who played the bachelor friend in a manner that was exactly right in every sense.[2] Terry's inspiration had certainly "paid off".

However, just before they played in *The Guardsman*, Lynn and Alfred took off for Europe to buy Lynn's

[1] E. W. Osborn, *Evening World*, New York, 14 October 1924.
[2] Stark Young, *New York Times*, 14 October 1924.

wardrobe with $6,000 which Lynn had saved up for just such an emergency, as the Guild gave her no money for this purpose. First, they went to Budapest to meet the author, Ferenc Molnar, to get his ideas on the playing of the piece. When they got to Hungary, they found no Molnar because he had run off to marry Lili Darvas. They never met him ever, at any time, although their names were always linked because of their fabulous success on stage and screen in *The Guardsman*. But, to get back to Lynn's purpose in going to Europe, they went to Paris to shop. At Paul Poiret's *atelier*, Lynn saw a model but the colour was wrong. She had it made up in white velvet— as anyone who ever saw her in it or a picture of her in it will never forget. It cost $1,000. They continued to buy and dine in Paris until time for the boat train. The result of all this was that Lynn had her wardrobe but they were penniless when they boarded ship with just enough money for tips to the stewards and a taxi home in New York. "We couldn't even pay the rent", Alfred smiled reminiscently.

A couple of days later Lynn gathered up her wardrobe and displayed it to Terry Helburn. Terry was delighted but pointed out she could only allow $50 toward each gown. "But if we run. . .", Lynn murmured. "If we run *ten* weeks", said Terry, "we will see what we can do." And they did and she did. However, in later successful Guild years she was allowed a lump sum for clothes, but Alfred said it was never enough—even though the $50 grew up to be $2,500 and more.

The 1925-26 season was opened at the Guild on 14 September 1925, with Philip Moeller's production of *Arms and the Man*. The presentation was so successful that the Guild determined to have a Shaw revival every year, which resolution they almost lived up to until Shaw's death in 1950.

The roles of Raina and Captain Bluntschli suited the Lunts well, as critics testified. "I believe that if Mr. Shaw had seen Miss Fontanne and Mr. Lunt put their good looks, their charm and their skill into the impersonation of his puppets last night, he would not, hereafter, be so coy to the amorous advances of the Guild."[1]

"Alfred Lunt and Lynn Fontanne remain paired here; as at home, as in the Guild's last season production of *The Guardsman*. Last night they did not divide the rewards of Shaw as equally as they did those subtleties of Molnar. Miss Fontanne, cute and personable as she gradually grew to be, had one moment of sore groping for her lines, a circumstance which future and more assured evenings probably will not duplicate. Neither she nor Mr. Lunt allowed the most innocent germ of travesty to fertilize during the semi-romantics of the first act. After that his peculiar aptitude for suave staccato absurdity became a high-strung treat. He has not the phlegm Shaw expected of his Bluntschli but perhaps you will be grateful for that."[2]

The roughhouse of the bedroom scene was grist to their mill and sheer delight for the audience. Their love scenes have always been one of their great points in acting. They believe that this is because they are so in love themselves, but it is much more than that really. Their movements are so deft and sure and so perfect and frequently so daring that they can raise the temperature of

[1] Percy Hammond, *New York Herald Tribune*, 15 September 1925.
[2] Gilbert W. Gabriel, *New York Sun*, 15 September 1925.

an audience in an unheated theatre in wartime. The late Vernon Rice, drama editor of the *New York Post,* was in London during World War II when the Lunts performed *Love in Idleness* at the Lyric Theatre in December, 1944. The Battle of the Bulge was on and the troops on leave were in sad need of cheering up. They wore overcoats in the theatre. As the love scenes progressed with Lynn in filmy décolletée (how did she endure the cold?), the temperatures of the watching GI's' Wacs, Waves, and other military personnel rose. Overcoats and even sweaters were shed as the imperturbable Lunts performed.

Arms and the Man was followed by their appearance in Lee Simonson's highly stylized scenic production of Franz Werfel's *Goat Song* which delighted the Guild subscribers with its earthy symbolism and was intended as caviar for the average audience. Brooks Atkinson in the *New York Times* of 26 January 1926 said: "Miss Fontanne's best scenes come in the last two acts; in the first act she appears more scornful of her vacillating bridegroom in her postures than in her speaking. . . As the restless leader of the insurgents, Mr. Lunt's acting has a smooth and varied flow."

They followed *Goat Song* in the late spring and summer with C. K. Munro's *At Mrs. Beam's.* This whimsical comedy did not enjoy a long run, but wilted in the early summer heat of 1926. It was during this run that the Arctic explorer, Vilhjalmor Steffanson, became so delighted with the light-hearted frolicking of the Lunts and Jean Cadell that he attended forty-two performances. The Guild box-office didn't have the heart to take his money after he had bought tickets nine times. That record must exceed that of any other fan of the Lunts in

enthusiasm and staying power. It is only rivalled by
the seventeen-year-old high school student who *stood*
through the nine acts of *Strange Interlude* nine times.
When the cast heard of this (Lynn was the original Nina
Leeds) they bought the youngster two tickets down front
and entertained him back stage at the dinner inter-
mission.

Concerning *At Mrs. Beam's,* the critics said: "Mr.
Lunt and Miss Fontanne have one grand gasp-producing
scene. They have done many things, though, that deserve
much higher praise."[1] "A second splendidly drawn character is that of the Brazilian lady assigned to Lynn Fontanne.
This time the actress slips as gracefully into the skin of
this fascinating tigress as she does into her silken négligée,
a bold bad lady with a fiery temper fairly exuding sex.
Alfred Lunt is the engaging thief. . . ."[2]

The 1926-27 season began for Alfred with Werfel's
tragic drama, *Juarez and Maximilian,* laid in Mexico
during Maximilian's brief reign, 1865-67. Alfred was a
superb Maximilian to Clare Eames' cool Carlotta, but the
settings seemed to dwarf the actors and the costumes
made them stiff. The critics were hostile. "To Mr. Lunt, a
facile player, was given the task of impersonating the
feeble Emperor who strove delicately to help the abo-
rigines of the Western hemisphere with European super-
vision. He seemed to be a very nice Austrian archduke,
'A little brother of his brother'. . . ."[3] "Alfred Lunt seemed
to me miscast".[2] "And Mr. Lunt, as Maximilian, might
learn a good deal from Mr. Daly's clean-cut enuncia-

[1] *New York Graphic,* 27 April 1926.
[2] Burns Mantle, *New York News,* 26 April 1926.
[3] Percy Hammond, *New York Herald Tribune,* 12 October 1926.
[4] Alan Dale, *New York American,* 13 October 1926.

1907   Wisconsin : The Rev. Robert Spalding in *The Private Secretary.*   (Amateur Production)

37

2

1918 Tour : George Tewksbury Reynolds III in *The Country Cousin* with
Alexandra Carlisle (Nancy Price)

1919 Hudson Theatre, New York : Clarence in *Clarence*

1923 48th Street Theatre, New York : Charles II in *Sweet Nell of Old Drury*

1923   48th Street Theatre, New York : Lady Castlemaine in *Sweet Nell of Old Drury*, with Laurette Taylor (Nell Gwynne)

1923   Ritz Theatre, New York : Ann Jordan in *In Love with Love*

1923   Ritz Theatre, New York : David Peel in *Robert E. Lee*

1924   Ritz Theatre, New York : Tom Prior in *Outward Bound*, with J. M. Kerrigan
(Scrubby)

1924 Garrick Theatre, New York : The Actor and the Actress in *The Guardsman*

1925   Guild Theatre, New York : Bluntschli and Raina in *Arms and the Man*

1926   Guild Theatre, New York : Juvan and Stanja in *Goat Song*

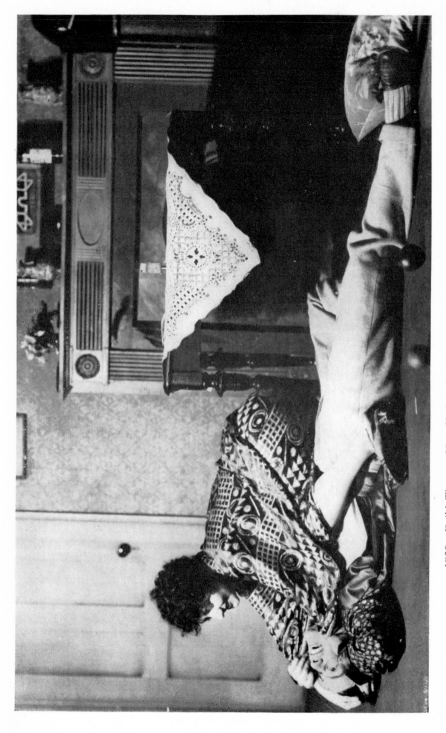

1926 Guild Theatre, New York : Mr. Dermott and Laura in *At Mrs. Beam's*

tion. . . Mr. Lunt seldom penetrates the obvious surfaces."[1]

In rehearsal the play had seemed deeply moving and the Guild thought they had another hit on their hands. They had to wait for this until November 1926, when the distaff side of this acting team appeared in a revival of *Pygmalion*. Her impish Liza caused Charles Brackett in the *New Yorker* to declare that "Lynn Fontanne's vibrant young Eliza Doolittle makes one's memory of Mrs. Patrick Campbell in the part seem like a faded cigarette-card. . ." Reginald Mason was an acceptable, if not exciting, Higgins. Henry Travers was a delightful Doolittle, the dustman. Contrary to public mis-memory, Alfred never played Higgins on Broadway, although he undertook it in repertory ou tour with Lynn in *Pygmalion, The Second Man, The Guardsman* and *The Doctor's Dilemma* a season or so later.

IV

W H I L E Lynn was busy at the Guild with *Pygmalion*, Alfred was heading the other Theatre Guild Acting Company at the John Golden Theatre in *Ned McCobb's Daughter* opposite Clare Eames. This was Sidney Howard's New England drama about bootlegging which was also the subject of a George Gershwin musical, *Oh, Kay!* starring Gertrude Lawrence that season. Edward G. Robinson, Margalo Gillmore and Earle Larimore also played leads in the Howard drama. Most of the actors played in two plays, some in three, on alternate weeks.

[1] Brooks Atkinson, *New York Times*, 12 October 1926.

3

About his performance in Howard's play, the reviews raved, "Alfred Lunt simply revels in the role of 'Babe' Callahan. He thrives visibly on the swaggering, the bullying, the rough jesting and the rollicking brutality that go with the part. Let the highbrows of the Guild constituency regret the fact as they will, this, their prized star, has found mighty easy and grateful the descent from the Hungarian or British classic to a Yankee carousel."[1] "Strangely metamorphosed since the close of *Juarez and Maximilian,* Alfred Lunt represented a wholesale bootlegger with unction, gusto and immense vitality. His was easily the finest performance of the evening."[2]

During the weeks Lynn was not playing *Pygmalion* she joined Alfred in Jacques Copeau's superb adaptation and production of *The Brothers Karamazov* with a cast which included Dudley Digges, George Gaul, Edward G. Robinson, Henry Travers and Philip Loeb. It was indeed a de luxe production with the great sincerity and impressive emotional direction of Copeau, the founder of the Théâtre du Vieux-Colombier, who influenced production in Western Europe and America in the years between the wars. The notices said, in part, "Mr. Lunt was exciting in these feats of impersonation and his display of Russian lunacy, overblown, unsexed, and unkempt was as convincing, I thought, as is his portrayal of Babe Callahan, the same bootlegger in *Ned McCobb's Daughter.* Miss Fontanne, of course, was bewildering as the beautiful Grushenka."[3] "Mr. Lunt comes off with the first honors, partly, no doubt, because he has the vivid role of Dmitri, but mainly for the insight and brilliance

---

[1] E. W. Osborn, *New York Evening World,* 1 December 1926.
[2] George Goldsmith, *New York Herald Tribune,* 1 December 1926.
[3] Percy Hammond, *New York Herald Tribune,* 4 January 1927.

of his portrayal . . . Neither of the two principal women has much to do, and the jobs were lavishly assigned to Miss Fontanne and Miss Eames, who did that little competently."[1]

In April 1927 the Lunts were given pure comedy again with S. N. Behrman's delightful *The Second Man* in which they appeared to great advantage with Margalo Gillmore and Earle Larimore. In November they were together again in the Guild's annual Shavian revival, this time *The Doctor's Dilemma*, with the fine full force of this distinguished acting company in support. The Guild might not have "starred" them in those days, but the public certainly did. The play had been opened in Chicago, contrary to the usual Guild custom of opening "cold". Earlier they had played *Arms and the Man* and *The Guardsman* there together, beginning their long affection for the Road no matter how exhausting it might be to them personally. This is why they are truly American stars, not mere Broadway stars as are so many others. After the New York opening Alexander Woollcott said of *The Doctor's Dilemma*, "It may be doubted if ever anywhere the crucial roles of the dying blackguard of an artist and his exalted, exalting wife have been so illuminatingly acted as they were last night by Alfred Lunt and Lynn Fontanne. It may be doubted if ever anywhere in our time they will be so well acted again. . . I should like to linger long over the almost phosphorescent quality of Mr. Lunt's performance, the gleam of his diablerie. I should like to write much of the dauntless humility of this all-conquering Jennifer."[2]

[1] John Anderson, *New York Post*, 4 January 1927.
[2] *New York World*, 22 November 1927.

Gilbert Gabriel recorded: "For, throughout the evening Miss Fontanne's performance is a clear-browed delight, understanding, warm, as alive as poised. Hers is infinitely better than Lillah McCarthy's playing of the part here in the Barker troupe. Mr. Lunt's Dubedat is vividly clever, too—the manners of Aubrey Beardsley attached to the looks of a young Sherwood Anderson, with the faun and the demigod exchanging compliments in his every expression."[1]

The Guild, having neglected the genuinely burgeoning talent of Eugene O'Neill, took to him with a vengeance in 1928. On 9 January Lunt created a *tour de force* in the title role of *Marco Millions* with Margalo Gillmore in the leading feminine role. This satiric comedy about Marco Polo, the Venetian merchant who journeyed to Cathay during the Renaissance, was brilliantly directed by Rouben Mamoulian and superbly designed by Lee Simonson. On 10 January 1928 Percy Hammond wrote in the *New York Herald Tribune*, "Mr. Lunt, who triumphs over a favorite's miscasting more than most good actors do, is in *Marco Millions* a resemblance of what Mr. O'Neill may have had in mind. From Sunday night's dress rehearsal rumors have come that he was not at his best in the role and that the performance suffered from his incapacities. But, to me, he was a legitimate caricature and as effective an implement in the character as Mr. O'Neill could hope for."

Alexander Woollcott said in the *New York World*, 10 January 1928: "I think, too, that it was O'Neill's achievement of a portrait by a mosaic of stencils that gave Alfred Lunt's performance a little the effect of

---

[1] *New York Sun*, 22 November 1927.

lapsing between each speech. It was, of course, a perfectly conceived and supremely competent performance, but it had only its one little moment of beauty in the first scene and it was marked by an almost hypnotic weariness, each line of the long role parting from him as if, although he was quite certain what the next might be, he had not quite decided whether to buck up and say it or just to curl up there on the Guild stage and take a good long nap."

On 30 January Lynn Fontanne first played Nina Leeds in the marathon O'Neill examination of the psyche, *Strange Interlude,* in which he used the old-fashioned asides of the eighteenth and nineteenth century theatre. These he called "thought speeches". Philip Moeller, the director, was at his wits' end trying to decide how to make the idea clear to the audience that these speeches were unheard by the other characters on the stage. He was returning by train from Washington when the air brakes were suddenly applied. The passengers were jolted into erect position and "frozen". Then Moeller saw what he could, should, and would do to make these speeches come directly without worrying the audience about the seeming unnaturalness of the other characters not hearing the words. He also followed the author's suggestion that the "thought speeches" be played at top speed. The action came through clearly to the spectators. The actors in the London company insisted on "acting out" all the speeches, which only slowed the production to a snail's pace and irritated critics and audiences alike. The author was blamed, when it was the fault of the actors.

Among the New York critics, Brooks Atkinson said in

the *New York Times* of 31 January 1928: "Lynn Fontanne as Nina and Earle Larimore as Sam Evans play with admirable distinction and resourcefulness. More than any of the others they have mastered the technique of this strange play; and without upsetting the flow of drama they contrive to give their 'asides' a true value. Meanwhile they describe two characters completely. One cannot speak too highly of their skill."

In the *New York World* the same day, Dudley Nichols, substituting for Woollcott who had resigned in a "pet" because he was not allowed to review a play which he had prejudged in a magazine article prior to its opening, wrote: "Miss Fontanne was superb. The most was required of her and she gave to the brim at every demand. She was possessed of an inward power which broke through every restraint as radium shoots its glimmering particles through everything that would contain it."

In December of the same year the Lunts were back together again in Philip Moeller's graceful adaptation of the Viennese Sil-Vara's *Caprice*. This comedy of love was, of course, beautifully mounted by Aline Bernstein and directed by Moeller. The costumes had been selected by Lynn herself in Paris the previous summer. The Guild allowed her $2,500, but as an assistant to the technical director, Kate Drain Lawson, I was present when Alfred was telling about Lynn's Parisian shopping spree with horror. Mrs. Lawson remarked that he was lucky to have that twenty-five hundred. Lunt's eyebrows went up as he replied, "Twenty-five hundred was nothing, not even a drop in the bucket." I can testify that her wardrobe was worth every cent paid as one who remembers with delight the white evening gown with an overdrape lined with red satin over the derrière which was impudently flipped at Alfred as she made her exit.

St. John Ervine was guest critic for the *New York World* at that time and he wrote on 2 January 1929: "It has not been my luck to see Mr. Alfred Lunt or Miss Lynn Fontanne act before. I shall esteem myself a very unfortunate fellow if I never see them again. Mr. Lunt's performance was a delightful exhibition of accomplished comedy acting: a fine and accurately observed show of manners. Miss Fontanne startled me with her brilliant artifice. I had not expected to see anything so good as this performance. Here was the essence of drawing-room, the very spirit of boudoir, the inner mood of elegant life.

"Miss Fontanne can rouse ripples of laughter by the way in which she plays on sentences—even full meaningless sentences, mere lumps of words clumsily thrown at each other. Such a series of gasps as 'oh-ah-I mean-but!'—on Miss Fontanne's lips becomes a piece of wit. Character flows into all that she says. Her mind works in every word. No wonder people are proud of this brilliant pair. They are destined to be prominent in the history of American comedy."

In the *New York Times* of 1 January Brooks Atkinson had written: "Nothing is finer pleasure than actors who have breathed so deep of a drama's spirit that they infuse every moment with life and vivacity. Miss Fontanne and Mr. Lunt are a matchless pair of volatile comedians. *Caprice* lives in their style of walking, their toying with boutonnières, and in their spontaneity with the line and colloquies. When they run their lines together they accent the meaning even while they confuse the words."

The perfection of the Lunts' performances are always

improved upon as the run on the play continues. On the closing night of *Caprice* in New York, Abe Kurnit, stage carpenter of *My Fair Lady* now, and then acting in the same capacity for the Guild, was standing near the Lunts before their entrance and heard Lynn say, "Alfred, if you do *that* and I do *this* at that point, I think we can get another laugh. Let's try it."

This paid off that night and again in London when they, along with Lily Cahill, Ernest Cossart and Douglass Montgomery, took the play to the St. James's Theatre. Alfred made his first London appearance on 4 June 1929, and Lynn made a radiant reappearance this time as a star.

S. N. Behrman's *Meteor* was written for them. It was a serious comedy about an egotist but was a trifle bitter for audiences still stunned by the 29 October 1929 stock market crash and not being anything but distrustful of Wall Street financiers. The fact that, in rehearsals, Behrman, who frequently had trouble with dramatic structure, tried to cram four acts into three did not help.

About the play, John Mason Brown wrote in the 24 December 1929 edition of the *New York Post*: "Even so *Meteor* holds its very real interests. And chief among these are the opportunities it gives Alfred Lunt and Lynn Fontanne and the manner in which they take advantage of them. Though it is Mr. Lunt who carries the burden of the evening—and carries it brilliantly—it is in the scenes when they are together that the acting reaches its sheerest perfection. For the Lunts play together as no other actors in our theatre do, with a fluency that is matchless, and an unselfish and precise sense of give and take which is a constant joy to watch."

The writing of *Meteor* posed a problem for the author, director and actors as they struggled to compress four acts into three. The end of the play was unfinished and at the dress rehearsal the director and the author had so heated a dispute that they both stormed out of the theatre separately and left the Lunts to their own devices. Alfred said to Theresa Helburn, "What are we going to do, Terry? We can't open." "But you'll have to", she answered, "we're completely sold out."

"So, on opening night we had no ending for the play and I was left with a long telephone scene. I said to the stage manager, believe it or not, that when I said the word 'schlemiel', he was to take the curtain down. That is the way we played it in Boston but we got it fixed up by the time we got to New York".

The next season was a more rewarding one for both the Lunts and the Guild. In *Elizabeth the Queen*, Maxwell Anderson wrote an historical drama of poetic nature which provided ample scope for them both. Lynn was truly regal as Elizabeth in a copper-coloured robe of a metallic material. She created a dynamic, autocratic and love-devoured queen with a simplicity of line which particularly became her. Lynn is a careful actress with her effects, she is never fussy. There is a leanness of line which is deeply appealing. It is a quality both possess which makes them decisive actors.

The role of Elizabeth's beloved Earl of Essex, who plotted against her tyranny, appealed deeply to Alfred and he was romantic, valorous, touching in his performance. On the opening night at the Martin Beck Theatre, on 3 November 1930, there were seventeen curtain calls, which is distinctly unusual because New York audiences are not given to lingering long after the curtain falls. It was a satisfaction for the actors and the Guild. Percy Hammond wrote in the *New York Herald Tribune* the next day, "Let us begin our journal this morning with a note complimenting Miss Lynn Fontanne for an impersonation of Queen Elizabeth so clairvoyant and so credible that it is likely to stand as the model of such things until she undertakes another." "Richard Lockridge in the *New York Sun* said: "Miss Fontanne, partially concealed by her really superlative makeup, has never been happier in a part. Every changing, flickering mood of a tempestuous woman is captured; the whole heartiness, absurdity, grandeur of the queen is in the playing. Mr. Lunt's part, a shade less difficult, nevertheless serves to bring out all those qualities which set him apart from the run of the actors." In the *Brooklyn Eagle*, Arthur Pollock wrote, "Never have Mr. Lunt and Miss Fontanne played with so great a fervor nor with so sure an effect, though they have done many roles and done them expertly, Their playing this time is something better than expert."

The next autumn the Lunts were back in the same playhouse in Robert E. Sherwood's light-hearted comedy *Reunion in Vienna*. This had to do with an Austrian archduke and the lady who was once his mistress but is now another's faithful wife. It was deliciously played by the pair with the able assistance of Minor Watson as the husband, of Henry Travers as the good-natured and querulous father-in-law and the incomparably, lusty Helen Westley as Frau Lucher (read Frau Sacher of hotel fame), hotelkeeper in Vienna and panderer to the wishes of the Hapsburgs.

There was a delightful bit of business where the

archduke picks up the beldame's dress and discloses her red under-drawers, gives her a slap on the bottom and exclaims, "Thank God, there's something in Vienna that hasn't changed." One night Miss Westley forgot to don her drawers, but Alfred imperturbably said his line with a straight face.

Of the performance Gilbert W. Gabriel wrote in the *New York American* on 17 November 1931: "Miss Fontanne and Mr. Lunt play it to the hilt. They play it swiftly, dashingly, humorously . . . and ornamentally. They revel in it, on tabletops and couches and canopied beds, to music, to cheers with the gusto and brightness to which they seem to have captured the key for all time."

John Mason Brown in the *Post* wrote: "When the Lunts are in topnotch form—as they generally are in comedy—there are no two players in our theatre who can equal or excel them. Their acting not only has a zest about it which is irresistible, but it has a precision equal to its energy."

After a long run and a tour in the Sherwood play, they joined with Noël Coward in the production of his *Design for Living* at the Ethel Barrymore Theatre under Coward's direction. This comedy about three people who love each other very much had attracted so much advance gossip that people paid black market prices for opening night tickets. Nor were they disappointed, for the three stars acted their heads off to the delight of their audiences. The engagement was severely limited to 135 performances and there was to be no tour, so that tickets were at a premium during the entire engagement.

In the *New York Sun* of 25 January 1933 Richard Lockridge commented: "They play with all the nuances, oddly coupled with exuberance which they have shown so often to our delight. And the whole, as written and acted, is as happy a spectacle of surface skating as one might hope to see. They skate with fantastic swoops and little nonsensical shouts and a fine abundance of animal spirits and sometimes on thin ice."

While John Mason Brown in the *New York Post* said: "It is the most brilliant comedy acting New York has seen in years. It is perfect in its smallest details, filled with unction which each of these players brings to the theatre."

As one on the other side of the footlights, Coward wrote in *Present Indicative,* "In *Design for Living* we all three gave the worst performances of our careers every night together for four months and managed to be very good indeed."

v

W H E N the Lunts went into joint management with John C. Wilson and Noël Coward in the production of *Design for Living,* the gossip columns stated that they had "broken with the Theatre Guild". But several times since they have appeared under the Guild banner or in a production jointly sponsored by the Guild and another management such as the Playwrights' Company when they did *There Shall Be No Night.* As late as the spring of 1957 Lawrence Langner said, "Alfred and Lynn haven't *left* the Guild. We have a gentleman's agreement that if we find a play suitable for them and they like it and want to play it, they'll do it. It is as simple as that. Certainly, they haven't left the Guild in the sense that newspaper columnists have sometimes implied. We've had thirty years of mutual benefit in working together. I hope we'll do it many times in the future *if* we can come up with a play all of us agree to do."

After closing this romp, Alfred and Lynn took *Reunion in Vienna* to London and the Lyric Theatre. Alfred staged the performance (his first attempt in that field) and they opened on 3 January 1934 for a run of 196 performances.

W. A. Darlington in the London *Daily Telegraph* of 4 January 1934 said: "I repeat that the acting of Mr. Lunt and Miss Fontanne in their play is high comedy acting of exquisite quality."

In 1935 they returned once more to Broadway and the Ethel Barrymore Theatre, this time in Noël Coward's *Point Valaine* which is the closest thing to a real failure that they have ever had. It was a rather revolting little play which was distinctly inferior Coward. The supporting cast was excellent, including Louis Hayward in his Broadway debut. The small talk was brittle and occasionally amusing but the particular triangle was not very rewarding to actors or their audiences. The show closed after fifty-five performances.

In the early spring they went into rehearsal for *The Taming of the Shrew* for the Guild and opened in Harry Wagstaff Gribble's hilarious production at the Nixon Theatre in Pittsburgh in April 1935. As Katherine and Petruchio, they opened at the Guild Theatre on Broadway on 30 September for a prosperous run of 129 performances. Richard Whorf, Sydney Greenstreet and S.

Thomas Gomez were in support. In his criticism in the *New York Evening Journal* of 1 October 1935, John Anderson said: "In a production so craftily put together there is scarcely any point in taking it apart. Mr. Lunt's, as Petruchio, is the outstanding performance, rich in its comic invention, full of energy and resource, tuned up to the finest pitch and done with superb and sustained relish. His mannerisms are gone and his voice, more flexible, touches the lines with sharp understanding and clear statement.

"Miss Fontanne without, of course, such a range in the part of Katherine, sustains a portrait of magnificent comic proportions and (in spite of serious injury to her knee) she matches Mr. Lunt's Petruchio with a shrew that is a shrew, a yowling, kicking, biting hellion projected into the play like a bat out of hell. Only once did she seem less than perfect and that in the long speech at the end of the play, which seemed lacking in vocal variety."

Burns Mantle in the *New York Daily News* the same day wrote: "In the playing, Mr. Lunt commands the evening. His Petruchio is a roistering delight, touched with a finer humor and given to less persistent swaggering than most. This Petruchio has his moments of being a little uncertain as to whether he will be able to master this clawing, spitting, biting Katherine or not.

"Miss Fontanne, clinging to her slightly Oriental make-up, is in full voice and a clamorous and boisterous shrew. It is not, I think, a style of comedy that suits her particularly, but she keeps Katherine well in character and accepts defeat finally not sweetly and softly as many Katherines do, but with a mental reservation that she still may have something to say about this business of being tamed."

This is a good point at which to document that ever present desire of the Lunts to improve their performances. Here are two notices of their return engagement of the *Shrew* in 1940. "Miss Fontanne's Katherine is a fiery spitfire and her appearance seemed to me to be toned down a bit. There was less of the Oriental suggestion in her facial make-up. . . . There is a sleekness and a vigor expressed in Mr. Lunt's Petruchio that are most satisfying. His added confidence and authority invite the hope that he may add still other classical revivals to the repertory of this, our finest acting couple."[1] And "The performances of the two stars have grown in richness and now Miss Fontanne's Katherine and Mr. Lunt's Petruchio must be placed among their most attractive charaterizations."[2]

In March 1936 they had their second successful bout with a Sherwood play, this time of a somewhat more serious nature but still a comedy, *Idiot's Delight*. The opening of this anti-war play was achieved in Pittsburgh, Pennsylvania, despite a national disaster. The Nixon Theatre in Pittsburgh is located in a tiny business section of that city at the confluence of three great rivers known as the Golden Triangle. The rivers passed the flood stage just before the opening. The basement of the playhouse was full of water and the streets leading to it were well nigh impassable except by boat, but the Lunts and the Guild decided to open anyway regardless of the weather and only hoped the audience would manage to reach the

[1] Burns Mantle, *New York Daily News*, 6 February 1940.
[2] Richard Watts, Jr., *New York Herald Tribune*, 6 February 1940.

theatre some way, George Greenberg, the stage manager, remembers.

The audience arrived, some in rowboats, and the play went well despite frantic improvising in the lighting because most of the equipment short-circuited. Next came the problem of transferring the play from Pittsburgh to New York for the Broadway opening. There was a state-wide embargo on freight, but telephone calls from New York to the Governor of Pennsylvania and to the officials of various railroad lines finally cleared the way. A special locomotive came in and the scenery, after being trucked through the flooded streets, was loaded on freight cars for a roundabout trip by way of Cleveland to New York.

Then came the frantic effort to get the actors and their trunks out of the hotels with all elevators out of commission. Some of the actors were on the twenty-second floor and so the stage managers, actors and whatever recruits they could draft among the hotel personnel moved forty trunks. With nation-wide front page publicity heralding their progress, the Guild company moved from Pittsburgh and made the hazardous return to New York in time to open as scheduled at the Sam S. Shubert Theatre.

In *Idiot's Delight* Alfred was playing Harry Van, travelling through Europe with a night club troupe called Les Blondes, who meets Irene, played by Lynn, a phony Russian, whom he remembers knowing somewhat intimately in the Hotel Governor Bream in Omaha, Nebraska, when he was with a mind-reading act. (This episode, expanded to a full-length play by two other authors, might just be called *The Great Sebastians*, if

1926   Guild Theatre, New York : Eliza Doolittle in *Pygmalion*

1926 John Golden Theatre, New York : Babe Callahan in *Ned McCobb's Daughter*
(R.). With Earle Larimore (George Callahan), Clare Eames (Carrie Callahan), Albert
Perry (Captain Ned McCobb) and Margalo Gillmore (Jenny)

1927 Guild Theatre, New York : Dmitri Feodorovitch Karamazov and Grushenka
in *The Brothers Karamazov*

Vandamm

1927   Guild Theatre, New York : Clark Storey and Mrs. Kendall Frayne in *The Second Man*

Messrs. Lindsay and Crouse don't mind.) Bretaigne Windust was given his first chance at directing this production under the guidance of Alfred and Lynn. Richard Whorf, Thomas Gomez, Sydney Greenstreet, Edgar Barrier, Francis Compton, Barry Thomson, Edward Raquello and Alan Hewitt were in the populous cast. Of the play, John Mason Brown wrote in the *New York Evening Post* of 25 March 1936: "But most of all it of course takes its place among the imperatives on any playgoer's list because of the superb manner in which it is acted by Lynn Fontanne and Alfred Lunt.

"In a blonde Garbo wig and some beautiful Valentina gowns, Miss Fontanne is as visually stunning as she is vocally satisfying. Her enigmatic Russian is a brilliant characterization, clear-cut and coldly fascinating. It comes as one more triumphant demonstration of her exceptional artistry.

"As for Mr. Lunt, he herewith takes his place among this department's favorite hoofers. He hurls himself ingratiatingly into his dance routines with a verve that is equalled only by his grace. He obviously enjoys spoofing the mannerisms of the floor show artists. And everyone enjoys him. But there is more than dancing to his performance. His hoofer is a deeply conceived creation. In spite of the gaiety he commands, he is poignantly projected and shows that Mr. Lunt has approached—and understood him—from within.

"The simple truth is that *Idiot's Delight* finds the Lunts at their topnotch best. Surely that is praise of the most superlative kind."

They closed the play on 4 July for a vacation at their beautiful and beloved farm, Ten Chimneys, at Genesee

4

Depot, Wisconsin, and reopened 31 July for 179 additional performances followed by a tour.

They were back on Broadway on 1 November 1937 for the Guild in Jean Giraudoux's high comedy about gods and mortals, *Amphitryon* 38, in an excellent translation by S. N. Behrman with music by Samuel L. M. Barlow. The prologue was scandalously amusing due to the construction of the clouds in Lee Simonson's design making Jupiter and Mercury appear to be reclining bare-bottomed. Lynn was the desirable mortal, Alkmena. Richard Whorf was Mercury. Sydney Greenstreet, Alan Hewitt, Barry Thomson and George Meader were once again in the Lunts' company.

The critics were again rhapsodic. Richard Watts, Jr. wrote in the *Herald Tribune* of 2 November 1937: "It is worth repeating that both Miss Fontanne and Mr. Lunt are delightful. Miss Fontanne looks very handsome in her Grecian robes and her playing never ceases to be gay and charming. Mr. Lunt, whether in the whiskers of Jupiter or the disguise of the absent Amphitryon, is invariably engaging, and in the moments when he is baffled by Alkmena's loyalty to her husband or annoyed by suggestions that the world he made is not perfect he is a complete joy."

Sidney B. Whipple said in the *New York World Telegram* the same day: "Alfred Lunt and Lynn Fontanne give their usual excellence to the production, which is, of course, only another way of saying that they are at all times fascinating, deft, and alive to every opportunity given them either in the script or out of their own imaginative minds."

The following March they opened in Stark Young's

fine translation of Chekov's *The Seagull*. Lynn was Irina, of course, and Alfred was Trigorin. Margaret Webster impressed the critics as Masha while Richard Whorf was a brilliant Constantine.

Brooks Atkinson wrote in the *New York Times* on 29 March 1938: "As Mme. Trepleff, the vain, selfish actress, Miss Fontanne cheapens the part considerably by overacting and by gaudily wigging it. As Trigorin, Mr. Lunt has the invaluable gift of making his lines sound as though he had just invented them on the spur of the moment. But he, too, seems a little obtuse to the spiritual solitude of the play as a whole."

On the same day, Richard Lockridge commented in the *New York Sun*: "Mr. Lunt's Trigorin is uncommonly varied and his long, central monologue is a brilliant exercise in the use of inflection and pause for the heightening and recasting of meaning. Miss Fontanne's Irina, is, of necessity, more typical, Irina being one of the characters less explored by the author. But she had a fine, bright time with the showy, amorally selfish actress."

In May they went to London to play *Amphitryon* 38 at the Lyric Theatre. In reviewing the Giraudoux Greek comedy, James Agate headed his review in the *Sunday Times* for 22 May 1938 with "The Lunts Have a Word for It". "The piece is beautifully acted". *Truth* for 25 May 1938 stated: "There is no one like Alfred Lunt. There is no one like Lynn Fontanne. Together they are indeed unique. Dialogue and characterization are almost unnecessary to them; their mere presence on a stage is an unending delight."

During the early rehearsals for *Amphitryon* 38, Alfred

71

arrived at the theatre in a great tizzy, the stage manager recalls, and called the company together for a talk. "Ladies and gentlemen, it is impossible for me to play this role, so we can not go on with this play. Please consider the production cancelled. Speak to the company manager and pick up your cheques. I can't go on. I can't find the green umbrella." He turned and left the theatre.

Lynn sat quietly down near the footlights and watched the perturbed actors who stood transfixed with dismay. Then she spoke, "Don't worry, we'll go on, and he will find it."

The rehearsal began and half an hour later, completely re-inspired by his respite, Alfred returned and raised his arm, announcing, "Don't worry. I've found it. We'll start again at the beginning of the act."

The exact origin of the green umbrella, meaning the inspiration for a role, seems shrouded in mystery. Noël Coward told Raymond Mander and Joe Mitchenson in June 1957 that the term dates from rehearsals for the repertory tour in 1927 which included *Pygmalion*, when Lynn suggested that he should use a green umbrella as Higgins, as he was depressed over his interpretation of the past. George Greenberg, many times their stage manager, was sure his first knowledge came at the time of the above incident in connection with *Amphitryon 38*. All members or former members of the Lunts' companies know the umbrella well.

After *Amphitryon 38* closed on Broadway, the Lunts spent the following seasons of 1938-39, 1939-40 touring from Coast to Coast in a repertory of *Amphitryon, The Seagull* and *Idiot's Delight*. They covered 30,000 miles in all and when they came back to town for the week of 3

February 1940, the Guild and John C. Wilson revived *The Taming of the Shrew* for the Finnish Relief Fund which was being collected by the Hoover Committee.

According to Burns Mantle, Robert E. Sherwood completed *There Shall Be No Night,* which had been inspired by a broadcast from Helsinki, two weeks before the special revival of *The Shrew.* Two months later the Lunts appeared in this eloquent drama, opening 29 April 1940 at the Alvin Theatre, produced by the Playwrights' Company in association with the Theatre Guild. This paean to the heroic Finns during the Russo-Finnish War of 1939-40 struck a great blow for democracy then and wherever it was later produced in whichever version. In the original version, Alfred appeared as a Finnish doctor, Nobel Prize winner, with Lynn as his American-born wife. They are distinguished professional people who represent intellectual thinking in a free Finland of 1938 after the Munich pact. Their son, beautifully acted by Montgomery Clift, is in love with Kaatri played by Elizabeth Fraser, daughter of a militarist family who suspect Russia of imperialism. We watch the effects of a Russian attack and applaud the Finnish resistance.

In the *New York Journal American* 30 April 1940 John Anderson wrote: Miss Fontanne is superb as the American-born wife of the Finnish scientist, and plays with a tragic perception as affecting and as sharply inflected as her sense of comedy. Mr. Lunt gives the part of Dr. Valkonen the sort of illuminated scientific touch that reveals the personal tragedy of a mind overwhelmed by brute matter, and he has also directed the performance."

Brooks Atkinson commented in the *New York Times* of the same day: "If Mr. Sherwood's craftsmanship is often uncertain, the Lunts' is unexceptionable. Aroused by the sincerity of their playing, they and their associates are acting it beautifully. Mr. Lunt, who was fooling with Shakespeare a while ago, looks the part of Dr. Valkonen straight in the face and acts it with impersonal sobriety and understanding, not forgetting to speak the contemplative passages with driving precision. As Mrs. Valkonen, Miss Fontanne plays with a light touch in the early scenes and a gallantry in the later ones that round out a completely articulate character. This is one of her finest characterizations."

VI

O N E of the most moving experiences that America had in World War II came before her actual entrance into the war. Over the National Broadcasting Company's nationwide network, Alfred introduced Lynn who read Alice Duer Miller's moving poem about beleaguered England, *The White Cliffs of Dover*, with a musical score by Dr. Frank Black. Miss Fontanne's reading was so highly acclaimed in the press and by word of mouth that a repeat performance two weeks later attracted millions to their radios. A recording of the broadcast was released and sold for the benefit of British War Relief.

In October 1941 *Candle in the Wind*, a war play by Maxwell Anderson, starring Helen Hayes, opened under Alfred's direction. This was the first time he had staged a play on Broadway in which he did not appear.

Evaluating Lunt's directorial efforts, Burns Mantle[1]

[1] *New York Daily News*, 23 October 1941.

wrote: "Alfred Lunt directed the play in something of the impressively serious mood and convincing realism he used with Sherwood's *There Shall Be No Night*. But in this instance he has permitted a kind of dull gray monotony to settle over the telling of the story which smothers it with set rather than human speeches."

Louis Kronenberger said in *PM* the next day, "Alfred Lunt's direction, it is true, seems somewhat over-reverent, making a slow play even slower."

In November, 1942, with great éclat, the Lunts opened in S. N. Behrman's *The Pirate* suggested by a play of the same name by Ludwig Fulda. Incidental music was supplied by Herbert Kingsley, gay costumes by Miles White and amusing scenery by Lemuel Ayers. In this charade Alfred apparently walked a tightrope with the greatest of ease to the delight of all audiences. Estelle Winwood, Clarence Derwent and Muriel Rahn supplied valuable support in this exquisite production. Alfred and his old friend, John C. Wilson, staged the play together. Dances were designed by Felicia Sorel.

Concerning *The Pirate*, Lewis Nichols[1] wrote: "And it is sufficient plot to set forth before the Lunts, for they can do anything. Miss Fontanne is roguish, coquettish, practical by turns. . . . Mr. Lunt can be bumptious or pleading, and, in addition to all that, he can break an egg to make an omelette and then find it turn into a rabbit. The man obviously has studied."

Louis Kronenberger in the 27 November edition of *PM* said: "The Lunts are in it up to their necks, for one thing and it would take more than just a dull play to dampen the spirits, or wreck the success, of the Lunts. . . . To

[1] *New York Times*, 26 November 1942.

get by with such fol-de-rol, you must have one of two things: a first-rate musical comedy score, or a lady and gentlemen from Genesee Depot, Wisc."

It is interesting to note at this point that in 1917, Alfred played "Serafina, [sic] a strolling player" opposite Cathleen Nesbitt as Manuela according to a playbill for the Pabst Theatre, Milwaukee, for the week of 20 August. This was Louis N. Parker's translation of Ludwig Fulda's comedy. Cecil Yapp, Ann Mason and Wallis Clark were also in the cast. The playbill is included in one of the scrapbooks in the Theatre Collection of the New York Public Library presented by Alfred Lunt and Lynn Fontanne.

After the run of *The Pirate*, they decided to go to London to act in Sherwood's re-written *There Shall Be No Night*. There was a strong reason for Lynn's decision. Though she had raised considerable sums of money for the American Theatre Wing of the British War Relief Society with her broadcast readings and recording of *The White Cliffs of Dover*, she felt that she must be on the spot as a born Englishwoman and Alfred naturally wanted to go with her. Since Russia at this time was England's ally against the Nazis, a play in which she was exposed as an aggressor nation would not be fitting, so Sherwood transposed the situation in the play to the German invasion of Greece and it opened that way at the Aldwych Theatre in London on 15 December 1943.

One night during the London run of *There Shall Be No Night* a bomb fell right next to the theatre and, as was customary, the fire curtain was lowered. Alfred called out, "Take it up, we're going on." The audience applauded. Lynn had been offstage awaiting her entrance

76

when the blast came. When she entered, Alfred's line was, "Are you all right, darling?" It was too apropos for Lynn, so she paraphrased until she could collect her senses and give the proper lines.

Terence Morgan, playing their son, was standing near the stage door and had disappeared. He had been blown out of the theatre; somewhat shaken, brushing the dust off his uniform, he reappeared on cue, smoothing his hair as he entered. This was wartime playing, indeed.

James Agate for the *Sunday Times* of 19 December 1943, wrote: ". . . . But perhaps Mr. Sherwood's greatest feat has been to fit Miss Fontanne with the part of the doctor's wife. This actress is a brilliant comedienne, a mistress of the art of insinuation, extremely skilled in the hoodwinkery of gestures of which Duse was the greatest exponent. Hoodwinkery? Well let me say the art of restraint suggesting the pent-up torrent, of avoidance hinting at virtuosity resisted. . . . On the other hand Mr. Lunt works by accomplishment rather than by implications. His fun is brilliant, his pathos is open and declared and at times unbearable. To sum I will say the play is lovely theatre."

A year later they turned to the dramatic gossamer of Terence Rattigan's *Love in Idleness* at the Lyric in London, which Alfred directed with great success.

Desmond MacCarthy, the British critic, wrote: "How beautifully they act together, these bright particular stars! Their passion for detail, for the right small gesture, the quick telling change of attitude or voice, her unfailing grace, his realistic sincerity, are as delightful as ever to watch."

After a considerable London run, they took the play

to the Continent to play for the troops before returning to America. The play was re-titled *O Mistress Mine* and had a fine Broadway run under the auspices of the Theatre Guild and John C. Wilson. The play toured the United States and Canada for two seasons. The executive director of the Theatre Guild, Theresa Helburn, caught up with a wonderful performance in Chicago and went along to sup with them afterwards in their apartment.

When Lynn crossed her knee, Theresa noticed a small bandage and inquired. Alfred replied, "Oh, she fell down in that blackout scene and skinned her knee. I was frightened, of course, but I couldn't help but think that just some day it might be a wonderful piece of business."

Of *O Mistress Mine,* Vernon Rice, critic for the *New York Post,* said on 24 January 1946: "Good old-fashioned magic returned to the theatre last night. Magic and fun and laughter. Alfred Lunt and Lynn Fontanne are home again. . . . The Lunts could stand with their faces to the wall reciting the alphabet in pig latin and if they wanted me to laugh, I'd laugh. If it were tears they were after, I'd shed them. Just putty in their hands, that's me."

In the *New York Times* that morning Lewis Nichols wrote: "The Lunts never have been better, gayer, more amusing. One swallow may not make a summer, but two Lunts can throw a great deal of weight on the credit side of what has not always been a good season. The welcome mat has been set out to good purpose this time."

It was not until November 1949 that they opened in a new play on Broadway. This time it was S. N. Behrman's *I Know My Love* adapted from Marcel Achard's *Auprès de ma Blonde,* which they played for 246 performances at the Sam S. Shubert Theatre under Guild-Wilson sponsorship and then played it for a year on the road.

This nostalgic comedy-drama about a successful marriage took place in a single setting, by Stewart Chaney, of a Boston mansion. The play opens in 1939 when the Chambers are celebrating their fiftieth wedding anniversary with their family. The play cuts back to show their development from 1888 on. The drama was a trifle thin and didn't have much bite. It was saved by superb acting and Alfred's suave direction, and it became as big a hit in New York as it had been in Paris.

Typical of the press comment was Ward Morehouse's article in the *New York Sun* for 3 November 1949: "Alfred Lunt, the world's best actor, is again playing love scenes with Mrs. Lunt, the brilliant other half of the theatre's first stage team and Broadway seems a wonderful place once more. . . . Alfred Lunt is again mumbling and sputtering, jerking his head and rolling his eyes as he explosively stalks Miss Fontanne, his prey for all of a quarter of a century, about the drawing-room. She is again gay and winning, taunting and knowing-arch, airy and elusive."

John Beaufort said in the *Christian Science Monitor* on 12 November: "It is hard to imagine how Alfred Lunt and his wife, Lynn Fontanne, could have chosen for their silver jubilee as an acting team a more appropriate play than *I Know My Love* . . . . Across the years, the Lunts and their admirers have taken the comic with the tragic. But high comedy is the foundation stone of the Lunt-Fontanne reputation. . . . Mr. Lunt's direction fills the responsively handsome Stewart Chaney setting with a whole procession of fine performances."

THE LUNTS

On 3 November, 1949, Howard Barnes said in the *New York Herald Tribune*: "Meanwhile Lunt has directed the work to perfection even when Behrman has been more intent on graceful prose than dynamic action."

VII

I N 1952 Alfred made his lone excursion into staging opera. In fact, he appeared in the opera himself and the work was *Così Fan Tutte* which opened at the Metropolitan Opera House on 28 December 1952. The next day, the eminent music critic Virgil Thomson, wrote in the *New York Herald Tribune*: Alfred Lunt opened the show by lighting the footlight candles. That was a gag. It was not a gag that he had directed the stage action of Mozart's *Così Fan Tutte*. Not before at the Metropolitan Opera House have I seen an opera so completely planned from a visual point of view, so charming and so thoroughly interesting from a visual point of view. . . . Mr. Lunt had, however, sat with the singers and their coaches in innumerable musical rehearsals. He knew the opera and he knew the cast when he came to direct them. The result makes history."

The *New York Times* critic, Olin Downes, said: "The twentieth century, or the last half of it, may well see this long underestimated and misunderstood opera, *Così Fan Tutte*, in a different light. Certainly Mr. Lunt has done so. His production appears to us in every way to serve a double and profoundly artistic purpose. It is comprehending of Mozart, and it is in the truest sense a modern realization of a classic masterpiece."

On 18 February 1954 Alfred's next venture in the directing field was unveiled by the Playwrights' Company at the 46th Street Theatre. This was *Ondine* by Jean Giraudoux in Maurice Valancey's English adaptation. Audrey Hepburn, Mel Ferrer, Marian Seldes, John Alexander, Peter Brandon and Lloyd Gough were all brilliantly on view, as were such former acting associates of the Lunts as Edith King, Alan Hewitt and William LeMassena.

Walter Kerr's criticism in the *New York Herald Tribune* of 19 February 1954 said in part, "Alfred Lunt has staged the eye-filling charade with enormous grace. The initial images are always stunning: a chess game gathering at the court, a strange trial on a rocky seaside, a midnight invasion of woodland sirens."

John Chapman wrote in the *Daily News* the same morning: "The production of *Ondine* has been staged by Alfred Lunt and once again this director of the Met's *Così Fan Tutte* demonstrates his instinct for creating beauty out of motion."

On 3 November 1954, John C. Wilson and H. M. Tennant Ltd. presented Alfred and Lynn in Noël Coward's much touted comedy *Quadrille* at the Coronet. They had originally appeared in the play at the Phoenix in London, opening September 1952. This play seemed a little like a re-write of *Private Lives* set back forty years in time. Edna Best and Brian Aherne were co-starred in America and Dorothy Sands and Brenda Forbes were brightly noticeable. It was a beautifully set show with lovely costumes by Cecil Beaton. Alfred's staging was extremely good, but even that and the superlative acting could not save a basically weak play, although it ran for 150 performances.

Mr. Coward did not fare well in the notices though his friends came off brilliantly. John Chapman[1] said: "But any play, even *Grandma's Diary* would be welcomed here if it had the Lunts in it—and the Lunts are back again, as handsome and slick and gifted as ever. It is an infinite pleasure just to watch Miss Fontanne pour tea, which she does twice, and to see Mr. Lunt knuckle his brow and pop his eyes, which he does several times."

Richard Watts, Jr.[2] wrote as follows: "It is an ancient statement about Alfred Lunt and Lynn Fontanne that they would be delightful to watch if they were reading the telephone directory, and there may have been cases when I have suspected that they and their audiences would have been better off if that had been what they were doing. . . . It is always a joy to observe them in action, not only because they are masterly performers, but also because they bring such style and relish to everything they do. . . . Nor is it a mere demonstration of brilliant stage personality that they offer, although that certainly is not missing. This is light, deft acting at its peak, even if the play is far from completely worthy of such artful playing."

With the run of *Quadrille* finished, an old friendship with Howard Lindsay and Russel Crouse bore fruit, *The Great Sebastians*. As we suggested earlier, this is the play that could have been based on a segment of the plot of *Idiot's Delight*. This "melodramatic comedy" opened

---

[1] *New York Daily News.*
[2] *New York Post*, 4 November 1954.

under the production auspices of the authors in January 1956 at the ANTA Theatre, the enlarged and considerably refurbished Guild Theatre in which they have had so many successes. Bretaigne Windust was once again in the director's seat. A vaudeville mind-reading act is playing in Prague and they find themselves involved in Communist political intrigue at a party after a performance. Their escape is accomplished only through their native wit and the longest kiss on stage that even Alfred and Lynn have displayed to audiences.

In the *New York Times* of 5 January 1956 Brooks Atkinson was of the opinion: "As usual, the Lunts are giving a bright performance in a dullish play. . . . Everything they do is meticulous, pertinent, fluent and funny . . . Golly, what they could do if they selected a script as subtle and skillful as they are!"

Whitney Bolton[1] wrote: ". . . and the Lunts, as even Patagonia must know by now, can take even thinner cotton and make it seem lustrous and delicious. The plainest of stories in the hands of these four individuals [Crouse and Lindsay] becomes something with the shimmer of magic and the shine of heaven. The most commonplace line takes on polish and intent, the merest situation takes on stature and delight. Since most of us go to the theatre to be conned, it is lovely to be conned by experts."

After a comfortable run on Broadway they did their usual Coast-to-Coast tour the following season, winding up in New York with a network telecast in a TV spectacular of the same play. Their debut in the new medium was hailed by all who saw the production and after their

[1] The *Morning Telegraph*, 6 January.

new success they returned once more to vacation at Ten Chimneys at Genesee Depot.

Whenever the Lunts hit Milwaukee on tour they are in Alfred's home territory, so the entire company is likely to be regaled with one of his superb dinners at Ten Chimneys, their farm in Genesee Depot. He prepares and even serves the dinner himself. Milwaukee is the company's favourite stop on tour. They like tours with Alfred and Lynn, anyway, because he spends as much time with the company in their railroad car as he does in the suite with Lynn—who spends her travelling time reading and thinking.

Although these tours are tiring, they are the reason why the Lunts are so very popular in their own country. The public knows that their beloved Lunts will be coming to them personally in their own theatres on the Road, not clinging to Broadway as so many stars do. They are accessible on tour and they have hundreds of friends who visit them back stage on the Road. Renewing these friendships seems to be another factor in keeping Alfred and Lynn young and handsome.

In May 1957 they returned to New York on their way to Europe, when I last talked with them. They smiled happily over the years of successful playing and marriage (they celebrated their thirty-fifth wedding anniversary on 26 May, just before they sailed). Lynn was at her most charming when she remarked : "There has been so much erroneous talk and so many rumours printed about when we were born and how old we are that I'd like to say one thing only—I wish I *had* been born on the day that I met Alfred and now I know I really *was* born then."

1928 Guild Theatre, New York :
Marco Polo in *Marco's Millions*

1927 Guild Theatre, New York : Louis Dubedat and Jennifer Dubedat in *The Doctor's Dilemma*, with (L. to R.) Ernest Cossart (Sir Ralph Bloomfield Bonington), Dudley Digges (Sir Patrick Cullen), and Morris Carnovsky (Dr. Schutzmacher)

4

1928 Guild Theatre, New York : Mosca in *Volpone*, with Ernest C o s s a r t (Corvine), Margalo G i l l m o r e (Columba) and Dudley Digges (Volpone)

1928 John Golden Theatre, New York : Nina Leeds in *Strange Interlude*, with Glenn Anders (Edmund Darrell, Tom Powers (Charles Marsden) and Earle Larimore (Sam Evans)

Vandamm

Vandamm

1928   Guild Theatre, New York : Albert von Eckhardt and Ilsa von Ilsen in *Caprice*

1929 Guild Theatre, New York : Raphael Lord and Ann Carr in *Meteor*, with
Edward Emery (Doctor Avery)

Vandamm

1930   Martin Beck Theatre, New York : The Earl of Essex and Queen Elizabeth
in Elizabeth, the Queen, with Robert Conness (Burleigh), Morris Carnovsky (Bacon),
and Barry Macollum (The Fool)

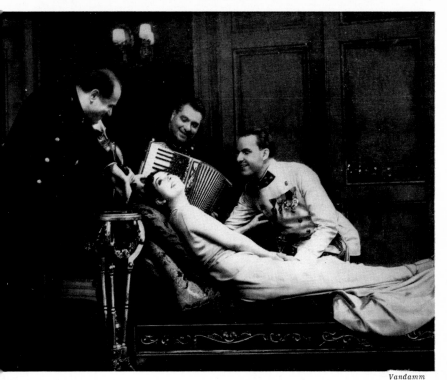

Vandamm

1931   Martin Beck Theatre, New York : Rudolph Maximillian von Hapsburg and
Elena in *Reunion in Vienna*

Vandamm

1933   Ethel Barrymore Theatre, New York : Otto and Gilda in *Design for Living*,
with Noël Coward (Leo)

1934 Lyric Theatre, London : Rudolph Maximillian von Hapsburg and Elena
in *Reunion in Vienna*

VIII SOME THOUGHTS ON ACTING

A F T E R more than thirty years of playing together, it seems generally accepted that the Lunts are the most superb technicians on the English-speaking stage as well as being emotional actors of the first rank. Laurette Taylor had excelled in the acting art and Lynn had grown up on stage under the watchful eyes of that great star. Alfred served his years of tutelage under E. E. Clive, Mrs. Langtry and Margaret Anglin, all great stars, directing stars, or directors in their own right.

In talking about her work with Miss Taylor, Lynn recalls, "Laurette never discussed acting technique with me. In fact the only time she ever said anything at all was in an early play. I felt *de trop* in one of her scenes and moved back to get out of her way. I moved right back when she hissed under her breath during the performance, 'Don't you dare upstage me!'

"It was the first time I had ever heard the term. I felt I was just doing the natural thing. I wasn't needed so I was getting out of the way. However, after that I watched her every move and patterned myself on her."

In speaking about themselves as a team, the Lunts say, "They say we are all tricks. What we do is exactly the opposite. We search for the truth and try to express it. We do the natural thing. Alfred in the beginning began occasionally playing with his back to the audience out of shyness and as a hangover from the amateur stage from

5

which he had graduated. We started overlapping our speeches because we know each other so well, it was the natural thing to do.

"This is not to say we don't exercise and experiment with technique. It is our weapon as well as our armour so long as we remember that the inner truth is essential. We always try to improve our performances no matter how long we run. One of our stage managers loves to tell a joke on us. The night of a play's closing on tour, Alfred made the customary little speech to the company and then said, 'Don't forget rehearsal at eleven tomorrow, now we can *really* start to work.'

"John Gielgud has always said to us that his bugbear was to have an actor standing in front of him, so Alfred for a week tried just that to see if it would hurt the comedy. We still say, if the line is funny, it will get a laugh.

"We've played around technically with a lot of things. Alfred and Douglass Montgomery were trying for two laughs in *Caprice* in London. Alfred used the 'handkerchief trick'. It killed *his* laugh but Doug's was twice as big. We left it that way.

"When I was first working on Bob Sherwood's *There Shall Be No Night,* I had to plump up the pillows on the sofa from the rear, which is always good business, but there was only mild amusement. Later I reversed myself, turned my back to the audience and bent over to plump them and it was a good substantial relaxing laugh which is needed in a taxing emotional drama.

"Once in *Arms and the Man,* I was worried because I wasn't getting my laugh. Lynn said, 'Why don't you try *looking* at me?' I did and got my laugh. It was right because it was the natural thing to do although I hadn't thought of it.

"In *Quadrille*, in character, Alfred asked for a cup of tea rather than the whisky which was the more natural potion for the part. The author had put it in for a laugh and Alfred thought it should amuse the audience, but it didn't. Lynn wryly observed, 'You aren't asking me for a cup of tea, you are asking for a laugh.'

"I did what she said and the laugh came naturally. Honestly, we are just the opposite of tricks. We play naturally and truthfully. We don't ever want to grow old-fashioned in our acting." They spoke together and the lines and the truth came across to their audience of one.

CAREER OF LYNN FONTANNE

STAGE

1905
26th December—
March, 1906

Appeared in *Cinderella,* pantomime by F. C. Burnand, Hickory Wood and Arthur Collins, Theatre Royal, Drury Lane, London

**1906—
1908**

Walked on in productions by Lena Ashwell, Lewis Waller and Beerbohm Tree. These include: *The Bond of Ninon* by Alfred Sutro, Savoy Theatre, London (Lena Ashwell), July 1906; *Monsieur Beaucaire* by Booth Tarkington (revival), Lyric Theatre, July 1907 (On programme as Viva Fontanne)

1909
January—
June

On tour as Rose Carlisle in *Lady Frederick* by W. Somerset Maugham (Dir.: Percy Hutchinson); and as Joyce in *The Peacemaker* by E. M. Bryant, one-act play produced as a curtain-raiser (Dir.: Percy Hutchinson) (Tour opened Theatre Royal, Bristol, 4th January)

11th
December

Appeared in *Where Children Rule* by Sydney Blow and Douglas Hoare, music by Edward Jones, Garrick Theatre, London (Dir.: Charles Rock)

1910
March—
May

On tour as Harriet Budgeon in *Mr. Preedy and the Countess* by R. C. Carton (Dir.: Weedon Grossmith)

23rd
June

Lady Mulberry in *Billy's Bargain* by Robert Lascelles, Garrick Theatre, London (Dir.: the Author)

September—
October

Toured Canada and United States with Weedon Grossmith as Harriet Budgeon in *Mr. Preedy and the Countess,* and appeared in the same part, Nazimova's 39th Street Theatre, New York, 7th November

1911
22nd
February

Gwendolyn in *The Young Lady of Seventeen* by Charles Brookfield, Criterion Theatre, London. Play in one act, as curtain-raiser to *Baby Mine* by Gertrude Mayo (Dir.: Weeden Grossmith). Production transferred to the Vaudeville Theatre in May

9th September—
1912
January

Mrs. Gerrard in *A Storm in a Tea-Shop* by Stafford Hilliard, Vaudeville Theatre, London. Play in one act, as curtain-raiser to *Baby Mine* (Dir.: Weedon Grossmith)

1912
February—
May

On tour with *Baby Mine.* (As understudy)

1913
January—May
and
August—
December

On tour as Gertrude Rhead in *Milestones* by Arnold Bennett and Edward Knoblock

THE LUNTS

1914

23rd
April — Liza and Mrs. Collisson in *My Lady's Dress* by Edward Knoblock, Royalty Theatre, London (Dir.: Frank Vernon)

31st
October — Gertrude Rhead in *Milestones* (revival), Royalty Theatre, London (Dir.: Frank Vernon)

1915

11th
February — Nurse in *Searchlights* by Horace Annesley Vachell, Savoy Theatre, London (Dir.: Holman Clark)

30th
May — The Governor's sister in *The Terrorist* by Laurence Irving, Playhouse, London. Sunday performance for the Pioneer Players, produced with the same author's *Godefroi and Yolanda* (Dir.: Edith Craig)

2nd
July — The maid in *A War Committee* by Edward Knoblock, a one-act play with an all-star cast at a charity matinee, Haymarket Theatre

12th
July — Ada Pilbeam in *How to Get On* by Edward Knoblock, one-act play in a variety programme, Victoria Palace, London (Dir.: Norman McKinnel)

29th
December — A Pleiade in *The Starlight Express* by Algernon Blackwood and Violet Pearn, music by Edward Elgar, Kingsway Theatre, London (Dir.: Lena Ashwell)

1916

March — Winifred in *The Wooing of Eve* by J. Hartley Manners, Lyceum Theatre, Rochester, New York (Dir.: the Author)

27th
November

Olive Hood in *The Harp of Life* by J. Hartley Manners, Globe Theatre, New York City (Dir.: the Author)

1917
27th
March

"Princess" Lizzie in *Out There* by J. Hartley Manners, Globe Theatre, New York (Dir.: the Author)

9th
November

Winifred in *The Wooing of Eve.* Liberty Theatre, New York

31st
December

Miss Perkins in *Happiness* by J. Hartley Manners, Criterion Theatre, New York (Dir.: the Author)

1918
5th
April

Bianca in *The Taming of The Shrew* and Nerissa in *The Merchant of Venice.* Special matinee performance, Lyric Theatre, New York

20th
May

Mrs. Rockingham in *A Pair of Petticoats* by Cyril Harcourt. (Succeeding Laura Hope Crews). 44th St. Roof Theatre, New York (Dir.: the Author)

9th
September

Mrs. Glendinning in *Someone in the House* by Larry Evans, Walter Percival and George S. Kaufman, Knickerbocker Theatre, New York (Dir.: Frederick Stanhope)

THE LUNTS

1919
16th
June

Mary Darling Furlong in *A Young Man's Fancy* by John T. McIntyre, National Theatre, Washington, D.C. (Dir.: Frederick Stanhope)

1920
1st
March

Anna Christophersen in *Chris* by Eugene O'Neill, Broad Street Theatre, Philadelphia, Pa. (Dir.: Frederick Stanhope)

3rd
May

Zephyr in *One Night in Rome* by J. Hartley Manners, Garrick Theatre, London (Dir.: the Author)

1921
20th
February

Dulcinea in *Dulcy* by George S. Kaufman and Marc Connelly, Cort Theatre, Chicago, Ill. (Dir.: Howard Lindsay) subsequently at Frazee Theatre, New York, 13th August

1923
18th
May

Lady Castlemaine in *Sweet Nell of Old Drury* by Paul Kester, 48th Street Theatre, New York (Dir.: J. Hartley Manners (Revival)

6th
August

Ann Jordan in *In Love With Love* by Vincent Lawrence, Ritz Theatre, New York (Dir.: Robert Milton)

1924
13th
October

The Actress in *The Guardsman* by Ferenc Molnar, Garrick Theatre, New York (Dir.: Philip Moeller)

1935   Ethel Barrymore Theatre, New York : Stefan and Linda Valaine in *Point Valaine*

1935   Guild Theatre, New York : Petruchio and Katherine in *The Taming of the Shrew*

1935 Guild Theatre, New York : Petruchio and Katherine in *The Taming of the Shrew*, with Doris Rich (The Widow), Sydney Greenstreet (Battista), Alan Hewitt (Vicentio), Horace Sinclair (Grumio), Bretaigne Windust (Tranio), Barry Thomson (Hortensio)

1936 Sam S. Shubert Theatre, New York : Harry Van and Irene in *Idiot's Delight*

1937 Sam S. Shubert Theatre, New York : Jupiter and Alkmena in *Amphitryon 38*

Vandamm

1938 Sam S. Shubert Theatre, New York : Boris Trigorin and Irena Arkadina in *The Seagull*

Vandamm

1940 Alvin Theatre, New York : Kaarlo Valkonen and Miranda Valkonen in *There Shall Be No Night*, with Montgomery Clift (Erik Valkonen)

Vandamm

1942 Martin Beck Theatre, New York : Serafin and Manuela in *The Pirate*

1925
14th
September

Raina in *Arms and the Man* by Bernard Shaw, Guild Theatre, New York (Dir.: Philip Moeller)

1926
25th
January

Stanja in *Goat Song* by Franz Werfel, Guild Theatre, New York (Dir.: Jacob Ben-Ami)

26th
April

Laura in *At Mrs. Beam's* by C. K. Munro, Guild Theatre, New York (Dir.: Philip Moeller)

15th
November

Eliza Doolittle in *Pygmalion* by Bernard Shaw, Guild Theatre, New York (Dir.: Dudley Digges)

1927
3rd
January

Grushenka in *The Brothers Karamazov* by Dostoevsky adapted by Jacques Copeau and Jean Coué, Guild Theatre, New York (Dir.: Copeau)

11th
April

Mrs. Kendall Frayne in *The Second Man* by S. N. Behrman, Guild Theatre, New York (Dir.: Philip Moeller)

12th
September

Opened tour of *The Guardsman* and *The Second Man*, Hanna Theatre, Cleveland, Ohio. *Pygmalion* added to the repertoire at Studebaker Theatre, Chicago, Ill., 26th September

31st
October

Jennifer Dubedat in *The Doctor's Dilemma* by Bernard Shaw, Studebaker Theatre, Chicago, Ill. (Dir.: Dudley Digges). Subsequently at Guild Theatre, New York (Dir.: Dudley Digges), 21st November

THE LUNTS

1928

30th
January

Nina Leeds in *Strange Interlude* by Eugene O'Neill, John Golden Theatre, New York (Dir. : Philip Moeller)

31st
December

Ilsa von Ilsen in *Caprice* by Sil-Vara, Guild Theatre, New York (Dir. : Philip Moeller)

1929

4th
June

Ilsa von Ilsen in *Caprice,* St. James's Theatre, London (Theatre Guild Production)

23rd
December

Ann Carr in *Meteor* by S. N. Behrman, Guild Theatre, New York (Dir. : Philip Moeller)

1930

3rd
November

Elizabeth in *Elizabeth, the Queen* by Maxwell Anderson, Martin Beck Theatre, New York (Dir. : Philip Moeller)

1931

16th
November

Elena in *Reunion in Vienna* by Robert Emmet Sherwood, Martin Beck Theatre, New York (Dir. : Worthington Miner)

1932

September

Toured the United States in *Reunion in Vienna*

1933

2nd
January

Gilda in *Design for Living* by Noël Coward, Hanna Theatre Cleveland, Ohio (Dir. : the Author). Subsequently at Ethel Barrymore Theatre, New York, 24th January

108

1934
3rd
January

Elena in *Reunion in Vienna*, Lyric Theatre, London (Dir.: Alfred Lunt)

25th
December—
1935
January

Linda Valaine in *Point Valaine* by Noël Coward, Colonial Theatre, Boston (Dir.: the Author). Subsequently at Ethel Barrymore Theatre, New York, 16th January 1935

23rd
April

Katherine in *The Taming of the Shrew* by Shakespeare, Nixon Theatre, Pittsburgh, Pa. (Dir.: Harry Wagstaff Gribble). Subsequently at the Guild Theatre, New York, 30th September

1936
January

Toured the United States in *The Taming of the Shrew*

16th
March

Irene in *Idiot's Delight* by Robert Emmet Sherwood, Nixon Theatre, Pittsburgh, Pa. (Dir.: Bretaigne Windust). Subsequently at Sam S. Shubert Theatre, New York, 24th March

1937
15th
February

Alkmena in *Amphitryon 38* by Jean Giraudoux, adapted by S. N. Behrman (Dir.: Bretaigne Windust), Ford's Theatre, Baltimore, followed by a tour with this play and *Idiot's Delight*. *Amphitryon 38* subsequently produced at Sam S. Shubert Theatre, New York, 2nd November

THE LUNTS

1938
28th
March

Irina Arkadina in *The Seagull* by Chekov, adapted by Stark Young, Sam S. Shubert Theatre, New York (Dir.: Robert Milton)

17th
May

Alkmena in *Amphitryon* 38, Lyric Theatre, London

1938—1939

Toured the United States in *Idiot's Delight*, *Amphitryon* 38 and *The Seagull*

1940
5th
February

Katherine in *The Taming of the Shrew* by Shakespeare, Alvin Theatre, New York (Dir.: Harry Wagstaff Gribble;

29th
April

Miranda Valkonen in *There Shall Be No Night* by Robert Emmet Sherwood, Alvin Theatre, New York (Dir.: Alfred Lunt)

November—
1941
April

Toured the United States in *There Shall Be No Night*

1942
25th
November

Manuela in *The Pirate* by S. N. Behrman, based on a play by Ludwig Fulda, Martin Beck Theatre, New York (Dir.: Alfred Lunt and John C. Wilson)

1943
1st
November

Miranda Vlachos in *There Shall Be No Night* (revised version) Court Theatre, Liverpool (Dir.: Alfred Lunt). Subsequently at Aldwych Theatre, London, 15th December

1944
20th
December

Olivia Brown in *Love in Idleness* by Terence Rattigan, Lyric Theatre, London (Dir.: Alfred Lunt)

1945

Toured the European Continent for Allied troops in *Love in Idleness*

20th
December—
1946
January

Olivia Brown in *O Mistress Mine* (*Love in Idleness*), Town House Theatre, Toledo, Ohio. Subsequently at Empire Theatre, New York, 23rd January 1946

1947—1949

Toured the United States in *O Mistress Mine*

1949
2nd
November

Emily Chanler in *I Know My Love* by S. N. Behrman, adapted from *Auprès de ma Blonde* by Marcel Achard, Sam S. Shubert Theatre, New York (Dir.: Alfred Lunt)

1950—1951

Toured the United States in *I Know My Love* (from October)

1952
15th
July

Serena in *Quadrille* by Noël Coward, Opera House, Manchester (Dir.: the Author, with acknowledgement to Alfred Lunt and Lynn Fontanne). Subsequently at Phoenix Theatre, London, 12th September

1954
14th
October

Serena in *Quadrille*, Colonial Theatre, Boston. Subsequently at Coronet Theatre, New York, 3rd November

111

THE LUNTS

1955
3rd
November—
1956
January

Essie Sebastian in *The Great Sebastians* by Howard Lindsay and Russel Crouse, Playhouse, Wilmington, Delaware (Dir.: Bretaigne Windust). Subsequently at ANTA Theatre, New York, 4th January 1956

1956—1957

Toured the United States in *The Great Sebastians*

FILMS

1924

Rose Bauman in *Second Youth* (Dir.: Albert Parker)

1931

The Actress in *The Guardsman* (Dir.: Sidney Franklin)

1943

Appeared in *Stage Door Canteen* (Dir.: Frank Borzage)

TELEVISION

1957
1st
April

Essie Sebastian in *The Great Sebastians*, live and in colour from New York on NBC-TV on a nation-wide network

George Freedley

CAREER OF ALFRED LUNT

STAGE

1912
7th
October—
1914

The Sherriff in *The Aviator* by James Montgomery, Castle Square Theatre, Boston, Mass. (Dir.: George Henry Trader). Weekly changes of bill, with the exception of a continuous run as William in *Believe Me, Xantippe* by John Frederick Ballard, January to March 1913 (Dir.: George Henry Trader)

1914—1915

Toured with Margaret Anglin's company as Alfred Courtlandt Redlaw in *Beverly's Balance* by Paul Kester; Col. J. N. Smith, D.S.O. in *Green Stockings* by A. E. W. Mason; and Orlando in *As You Like It* by Shakespeare

August

Toured in vaudeville as John Belden in a one-act version of *Her Husband's Wife* by A. E. Thomas, with Laura Hope Crews. Philadelphia and Washington

August—
September

Appeared in *Iphigenia* in *Tauris* by Euripides, and in *Electra* and *Medea* by Sophocles, the Greek Theatre, Berkeley, Calif.

1916
4th
June

Jacques in *As You Like It*, Municipal Open Air Theatre, St. Louis, Missouri

113

8th September	Fred Fowler in *Ashes* by Percy Fendall, Orpheum Theatre, San Francisco, Calif. (Vaudeville tour with Mrs. Langtry)
12th November	Eric Huntsdowne in *The Eleventh Hour* by Edgar Allan Wolfe (Vaudeville tour with Mrs. Langtry)
1917 20th August	Trillo in *The Pirate* by Ludwig Fulda, translation by Louis N. Parker, Pabst Theatre, Milwaukee, Wisconsin (Dir.: George Foster Platt)
17th October	Claude Estabrook in *Romance and Arabella* by William Hurlbut, Harris Theatre, New York (Dir.: George Foster Platt)
1918	Toured as George Tewksbury Reynolds III in *The Country Cousin* by Booth Tarkington and Julian Street
1919 20th September	The title role in *Clarence* by Booth Tarkington, Hudson Theatre, New York (Dir.: Frederick Stanhope)
1920—1921	Toured in *Clarence*
8th November	Ames in *The Intimate Strangers* by Booth Tarkington, Henry Miller Theatre, New York (Dir.: Ira Hards)

1943 Aldwych Theatre, London : Karilo Valchos and Miranda Valchos in *There Shall Be No Night*

Cecil Beaton

1944   Lyric Theatre, London : Sir John Fletcher and Olivia Brown in *Love in Idleness*

1946 Empire Theatre, New York : Sir John Fletcher and Olivia Brown in
O, Mistress Mine

1949 Sam S. Shubert Theatre, New York : Thomas Chanler and Emily Chanler in
I Know My Love

1949   Sam S. Shubert Theatre, New York : Thomas Chanler and Emily Chanler in
I Know My Love

Cecil Beaton

1952   Phoenix Theatre, London :   Axel Diensen and Serena in *Quadrille,* with
Griffith Jones (Hubert) and Marian Spencer (Charlotte)

1954 Coronet Theatre, New York : Axel Diensen and Serena in *Quadrille*, with
Brian Aherne (Hubert) and Edna Best (Charlotte)

Vandamm

1956 ANTA Theatre, New York : Rudi Sebastian and Essie Sebastian in *The Great Sebastians*, with Simon Oakland (Sergeant Javorsky)

Vandamm

1956   ANTA Theatre, New York : Rudi Sebastian and Essie Sebastian in *The Great Sebastians*, with Simon Oakland (Sergeant Javorsky)

1923   Film : John Thorne in *Backbone*, with Edith Roberts

1923   Film : Howard Spurlock in *The Ragged Edge*, with Mimi Palmeri and
Wallace Erskine

1924   Film : Roland Francis in *Second Youth,* with Mimi Palmeri

1931   Film : The Actor and the Actress in *The Guardsman*

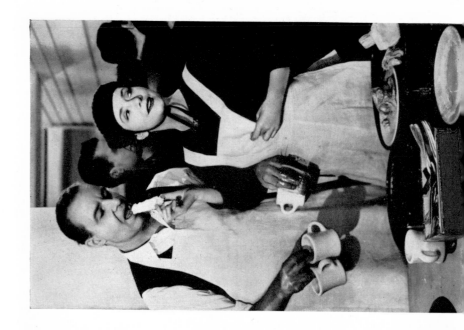

1931 Film : The Actor and the Actress in *The Guardsman*

Metro-Goldwyn-Mayer

1943 Film : As Themselves, in *Stage Door Canteen*

Metro-Goldwyn-Mayer

1922
20th
September

Count Alexandre de Lussac in *Banco* by Alfred Savoir, adapted by Clare Kummer, Ritz Theatre, New York (Dir.: Robert Milton)

1923
18th
May

Charles II in *Sweet Nell of Old Drury* by Paul Kester, (Revival) 48th St. Theatre, New York (Dir.: J. Hartley Manners)

20th
November

David Peel in *Robert E. Lee* by John Drinkwater, Ritz Theatre, New York (Dir.: Robert Milton)

1924
6th
January

Tom Prior in *Outward Bound* by Sutton Vane, Ritz Theatre, New York (Dir.: Robert Milton)

13th
October

The Actor in *The Guardsman* by Ferenc Molnar, Garrick Theatre, New York (Dir.: Philip Moeller)

1925
14th
September

Bluntschli in *Arms and the Man* by Bernard Shaw, Guild Theatre, New York (Dir.: Philip Moeller)

1926
25th
January

Juvan in *Goat Song* by Franz Werfel, Guild Theatre, New York (Dir.: Jacob Ben-Ami)

26th
April

Mr. Dermott in *At Mrs. Beam's* by C. K. Munro, Guild Theatre, New York (Dir.: Philip Moeller)

127

6

11th
October

Maximilian in *Juarez* and *Maximilian* by Franz Werfel, Guild Theatre, New York (Dir.: Philip Moeller)

29th
November

Babe Callahan in *Ned McCobb's Daughter* by Sidney Howard, John Golden Theatre, New York (Dir.: Philip Moeller)

1927
3rd
January

Dmitri in *The Brothers Karamazov* by Dostoevsky, adapted by Jacques Copeau and Jean Coué, Guild Theatre, New York (Dir.: Copeau)

11th
April

Clark Storey in *The Second Man* by S. N. Behrman, Guild Theatre, New York (Dir.: Philip Moeller)

12th
September

Opened tour of *The Guardsman* and *The Second Man,* Hanna Theatre, Cleveland, Ohio

26th
September

Henry Higgins in *Pygmalion* (added to the repertoire) Studebaker Theatre, Chicago, Ill.

31st
October

Louis Dubedat in *The Doctor's Dilemma* by Bernard Shaw, Studebaker Theatre, Chicago, Ill. (Dir.: Dudley Digges). Subsequently at the Guild Theatre, New York, 21st November

1928
9th
January

Marco Polo in *Marco Millions* by Eugene O'Neill, Guild Theatre, New York (Dir.: Rouben Mamoulian)

9th
April

Mosca in *Volpone* by Stefan Zweig based on Ben Jonson, Guild Theatre, New York (Dir.: Philip Moeller)

128

31st December	Albert von Eckhardt in *Caprice* by Sil-Vara, Guild Theatre, New York (Dir.: Philip Moeller)
1929 4th June	Albert von Eckhardt in *Caprice*, St. James's Theatre, London (Theatre Guild Production)
23rd December	Raphael Lord in *Meteor* by S. N. Behrman, Guild Theatre, New York (Dir.: Philip Moeller)
1930 3rd November	Essex in *Elizabeth, the Queen* by Maxwell Anderson, Martin Beck Theatre, New York (Dir.: Philip Moeller)
1931 16th November	Rudolph Maximillian von Hapsburg in *Reunion in Vienna* by Robert Emmet Sherwood, Martin Beck Theatre, New York (Dir.: Worthington Miner)
1932 September	Toured the United States in *Reunion in Vienna*
1933 3rd January	Otto in *Design for Living* by Noël Coward, Hanna Theatre Cleveland, Ohio (Dir.: the Author). Subsequently at Ethel Barrymore Theatre, New York, 24th January
1934 3rd January	Rudolph Maximillian von Hapsburg in *Reunion in Vienna*, Lyric Theatre, London (Dir.: Alfred Lunt)

129

THE LUNTS

25th
December—
1935
January

Stefan in *Point Valaine* by Noël
Coward, Colonial Theatre Boston (Dir.:
the Author). Subsequently at Ethel
Barrymore Theatre, New York, 11th
January 1935

23rd
April

Petruchio in *The Taming of the Shrew*
by Shakespeare, Nixon Theatre, Pittsburgh, Pa. (Dir.: Harry Wagstaff
Gribble). Subsequently at Guild
Theatre, New York, 30th September

1936
January—

Toured the United States in *The Taming of the Shrew*

16th
March

Harry Van in *Idiot's Delight* by Robert
Emmet Sherwood, Nixon Theatre, Pitts-
burgh, Pa. (Dir.: Bretaigne Windust).
Subsequently at Sam S. Shubert
Theatre, New York, 24th March

1937
15th
February

Jupiter in *Amphitryon 38* by Jean
Giraudoux, adapted by S. N. Behrman
(Dir.: Bretaigne Windust), Ford's
Theatre, Baltimore. Followed by a
tour with this play and *Idiot's Delight*.
Amphitryon 38 subsequently produced
Sam S. Shubert Theatre, New York,
2nd November

1938
28th
March

Trigorin in *The Seagull* by Chekov,
adapted by Stark Young, Sam S.
Shubert Theatre, New York (Dir.:
Robert Milton)

17th
May

Jupiter in *Amphitryon* 38, Lyric
Theatre, London

1938—1939

Toured the United States in *Idiot's Delight, Amphitryon* 38, and *The Seagull*

1940
5th
February

Petruchio in *The Taming of the Shrew* by Shakespeare, Alvin Theatre, New York (Dir.: Harry Wagstaff Gribble)

29th
April

Kaarlo Valkonen in *There Shall Be No Night* by Robert E. Sherwood, Alvin Theatre, New York (Dir.: Alfred Lunt)

November—
1941
April

Toured the United States in *There Shall Be No Night*

22nd
October

Directed *Candle in the Wind* by Maxwell Anderson, Sam S. Shubert Theatre, New York.

1942
25th
November

Serafin in *The Pirate* by S. N. Behrman, based on the play by Ludwig Fulda, Martin Beck Theatre, New York (Dir.: Alfred Lunt and John C. Wilson)

1943
1st
November

Karilo Valchos in *There Shall Be No Night* (revised version), Court Theatre, Liverpool (Dir.: Alfred Lunt). Subsequently at Aldwych Theatre, London, 15th December

1944
20th
December

Sir John Fletcher in *Love in Idleness* by Terence Rattigan, Lyric Theatre, London (Dir.: Alfred Lunt)

1945

Toured the European Continent for Allied troops in *Love in Idleness*

20th
December—
1946
January

Sir John Fletcher in *O Mistress Mine* (*Love in Idleness*) Town Hall Theatre, Toledo, Ohio (Dir.: Alfred Lunt). Subsequently at Empire Theatre, New York, 23rd January 1946

1947—1949

Toured the United States in *O Mistress Mine*

1949
2nd
November

Thomas Chanler in *I Know My Love* by S. N. Behrman, adapted from *Auprès de ma Blonde* by Marcel Achard, Sam S. Shubert Theatre, New York (Dir.: Alfred Lunt)

1950—1951

Toured the United States in *I Know My Love*

1951
28th
December

Directed and walked on in *Così Fan Tutte*, opera by Mozart, Metropolitan Opera House, New York

1952
15th
July

Axel Diensen in *Quadrille* by Noël Coward, Opera House, Manchester, (Dir.: the Author, with acknowledgement to Alfred Lunt and Lynn Fontanne). Subsequently at Phoenix Theatre, London, 12th September

1954
3rd
February

Directed *Ondine* by Jean Giraudoux, adapted by Maurice Valancey, 46th St. Theatre, New York

14th
October

Axel Diensen in *Quadrille,* Colonial Theatre, Boston. Subsequently at Coronet Theatre, New York, 3rd November

1955
3rd
November—
1956
January

Rudi Sebastian in *The Great Sebastians* by Howard Lindsay and Russel Crouse, Playhouse, Wilmington, Del. (Dir.: Bretaigne Windust). Subsequently at ANTA Theatre, New York, 4th January 1956

1956—1957

Toured the United States in *The Great Sebastians*

FILMS

1923

Howard Spurlock in *The Ragged Edge* (Dir.: Harman Weight)

John Thorne and André de Mersay in *Backbone* (Dir.: Edward Sloman)

1924

Roland Francis in *Second Youth* (Dir.: Albert Parker)

1931

The Actor in *The Guardsman* (Dir.: Sidney Franklin)

1943

Appeared in *Stage Door Canteen* (Dir.: Frank Borzage)

THE LUNTS

1957
1st
April

The Great Sebastians, live in colour, NBC-TV nation-wide network, from New York

PRODUCTIONS DIRECTED

1934

Reunion in Vienna, London only

1940 and 1943

There Shall Be No Night, New York and London

1941

Candle in the Wind, New York

1942

The Pirate (with J. C. Wilson)

1944

Love in Idleness (O Mistress Mine), London and New York

1949

I Know My Love, New York

1951

Così Fan Tutte, New York

1952 and 1954

Quadrille, London and New York
Cosi Fan Tutte, New York
(with Lynn Fontanne and Noël Coward)

1954

Ondine, New York